BOWLING THROUGH INDIA

THIS BOOK IS NOT DEDICATED
TO REECE AND STEW, WHO WILL ALSO
NOT GET A CENT OF THE PROCEEDS
(BECAUSE THEY'RE BLUDGERS).

RANDOM HOUSE
NEW ZEALAND

BOWLING THROUGH INDIA

FIVE KIWI BLOKES
TAKE ON INDIA AT CRICKET

JUSTIN BROWN • PHOTOGRAPHY BY BRENDON O'HAGAN

PAKISTAN

CHINA

NEPAL

DELHI

JAIPUR

AGRA

BHUTAN
DARJELING

ORCHA

VARANASI

KOLKATA BANGLADESH

INDIA

MYANMAR

BAY OF BENGAL

MUMBAI

ARABIAN
SEA

THE BLACK CRAPS'
TRAIL OF DESTRUCTION

CONTENTS

Previous page: The Maidan (meaning 'open field') is the largest urban park in Kolkata. Historically, it has been used for political rallies, army parades and book fairs, but on Sundays it's all about cricket.

FIVE IN A BILLION

ost men, when away from chores and loved ones, choose to fish or golf, a jaunt that typically culminates in late-night drinking sessions and regret. The only proof they were away at all is a hangover the size of Texas and a similarly hefty credit-card bill.

While these trips are a great way to clear the cobwebs, sometimes what a bloke really needs is a shock to the system. A comfort-zone upheaval. A new battery instead of a recharge. A change instead of a holiday.

Such a plan was currently being discussed by the Black Craps, a team of backyard cricketers, as they munched on stale buns and told lies on a flight from Auckland to Singapore, and ultimately Kolkata. Actually, that's not entirely true: three of the Black Craps — those who could afford only economy — were consuming the buns. The other two, already having created a rift in the team, opted for business class, quaffing champagne and perving at air hosties. Even so, you'd think the trio in economy would have been quietly respectful of their wealthier, better-dressed, 'served before cattle class' counterparts. That would have been the right thing to do. That would have been dignified and admirable. Sadly, however, that wasn't the case at all.

We were blokes. And we were jealous.

We took the piss out of them for the whole trip.

Speaking of the trip, this was the goal: to play backyard cricket with Indians in their own backyard. Every effort would be made to play by their rules, unless we happened to be losing. In our gear bag were five white knitted vests, twenty Auckland Aces cricket caps (for gifts) and an official scorebook. We carried no bats or balls, trusting a cricket-crazy nation like India to supply us with the most rudimentary equipment (mostly to accommodate our skill level). And this was the team:

JUSTIN BROWN — ECONOMY

The other Black Craps will be upset I'm first on the list, but I'm the writer and there's little they can do about it. Much to my team's disgust, I was carrying an injury into the series. Three weeks before departure, I dropped a laptop on my bare left foot at 4.45 am. It fell from waist height directly onto my big toe, acting a little like a blunt guillotine. Choice words were chosen.

I was also at that time a breakfast radio host, but don't hold that against me. And I've written a few books. More interestingly, for this trip in any case, I'm a retired opening batsman for the Horowhenua Third XI and an intercontinental sleepwalker.

The blind leading the blind. The Black Craps (from left) Reece Irving, John Bougen (with weapon), the author, Stew Gunn and Brendon O'Hagan.

JOHN BOUGEN — BUSINESS CLASS

Businessman, farmer and photographer and author of, among other books, *An Absolutely Outrageous Adventure, Made in Morocco, Taking Tea in the Medina* and *My Dream*. He holds a world record for travelling to the most countries in the least amount of time — 191 nations in 167 days.

John sat in business class, but in all fairness he deserved to: he's made his money and enjoys the finer things in life. He once said, 'When you get on a plane, never turn right.' It was to John that I stupidly mentioned the idea of this trip over drinks one winter's evening. One thing about John: he never turns down a challenge — or a good time, which is probably why he has spent the past few years working on a farm in the South Island high country.

BRENDON O'HAGAN — ECONOMY

Brendon is the poor bugger who took fourteen thousand photos while the rest of us smacked sixes over cowpats and almost got arrested in Mumbai. He has been a professional photographer (not bail bondsman) for fifteen years, although this was to be the first time away from his young family. This became quite obvious as he

crammed in as many movies as possible on the first leg of the flight.

Brendon has taken photos of some of the world's leading sportsmen, although this didn't impress the Black Craps one iota. As long as we could scrounge a free photo album off him at the conclusion of the trip, he could stay.

Note: Brendon may have a good eye, but he doesn't exactly have a cast-iron stomach: he had the shits before reaching Singapore.

REECE IRVING — ECONOMY

The saying 'Take half the clothes and twice the money' was written for Reece (except for the money part: he took none). I have never known anyone pack so little, yet change three times daily (in clothes we had never seen!).

The first time Brendon and I met Reece was at passport control in Auckland. We sniggered at his hobo-looking blanket, firmly strapped to his one and only (carry-on, at that) bag. But he was more experienced than us; later, we would be the ones freezing our nads off in Tenzing Norgay's home town.

Reece, a chronic snorer, is a former tour guide for the Trans-Siberian Railway, having completed it 26 times. ('I get bored easily, that's why I stopped.') He also speaks perfect Hindi, as a result of living in Varanasi when he was twenty. (He once drank his own urine for six months as part of a yoga course, too, but more on that later.)

Early resentment was directed at Reece (especially by Brendon and me) for, although he was sitting in economy like us, his whole trip was being paid for by John because, said John, 'He's my cousin's cousin and he speaks Hindi'.

Likely story.

STEW GUNN — BUSINESS CLASS

The other bludger. A farmer from the South Island, Stew was a last-minute ring-in for author/philanthropist/farmer Christine Fernyhough, who was trampled by a heifer six weeks before departure. Christine ended up with a badly broken leg, and Stew ended up with a trip to India.

Alas, this wasn't to be the only free lunch Stew would score, as we were soon to discover. Here was a man who had no problem not paying. In fact, he had it down to a fine art.

'When I asked John whether he wanted a contribution towards the trip,' he beamed, sinking another double G and T, 'he said, "No, but if I ever see you not fucking smiling, you're going home!"'

Stew is also John Wright's cousin, which would ultimately come in very handy because the former India coach is treated like the proverbial holy cow all over India.

Capital of the British Raj (and the so-called Jewel in the Crown) until 1912, Kolkata is now considered the poor cousin of India's great cities (Delhi, Mumbai, Chennai and now Bangalore). Once a regal metropolis filled with sprawling Victorian monuments, in the cold light of day the old girl looks ready to crumble at any minute.

So John and Stew sat up the front while Reece, Brendon and I got to know each other down the back of the bus. I was glad Brendon was sitting next to Reece, who was fresh from pulling an all-nighter, having just finished his last exam of the year.

'I barely had time for bacon and eggs and a shower before the taxi arrived at 6 am,' Reece said, knocking back a pint of water.

'So you won't join me for a Bloody Mary then?' I asked.

Reece shook his head. Brendon didn't stir. He wasn't listening. He had already watched *Transformers* and was on to *The Bourne Identity*.

'Since you spent so much time in India, could you enlighten me about

Bollywood movies?' I said, flicking through the in-flight TV guide. With only eighty-one movies to choose from I was desperate to make the right decision, my only other option being to start reading *Shantaram*, a nine-hundred-page epic about an escaped convict-turned-Mumbai slum doctor.

'Here's how your typical Bollywood movie goes,' Reece said with a glint in his eye. 'Good guy, bad guy, both after the same woman. Bad guy gets the girl first. Good guy rescues woman. Seven songs — there's always seven songs. Then there's the wet sari scene, then the "dancing around the tree" scene. No kissing — there's never any kissing — and it always ends with a wedding.'

'Right,' I said. 'Think I'll read my book.'

SINGAPORE.

Boring. Clean. No cricket. Reece snored.

KOLKATA

When we arrived, fresh from the pristine streets of Singapore, there was a distinct chill in the night air. Nobody told us India would be cold. Reece, whom we had ridiculed in the Auckland summer, smugly wrapped his Northern Himalayan blanket around his shoulders and smiled.

'Blanket Boy,' we all muttered.

'Warm Blanket Boy,' he replied.

On the ride from the airport to the hotel we were wide-eyed and weary. We stared, we shook our heads, we jabbered away like toddlers the night before Christmas. Locals honked and honked as if repetition earned rupees. Indeed, just as using a horn at home signified something drastically wrong, using no horn at all in Kolkata appeared to have the same effect.

At the first set of traffic lights we saw our first beggar, a teary-eyed woman putting her hand to her mouth. A baby, not looking entirely unhappy, glared at the strange vehicle with its equally strange white folk.

'Last time I was here,' said Reece, looking longingly at the cluttered, chaos-filled streets, 'the beggars were on strike.'

'What?' we all asked, trying our best not to reach for our pockets, knowing that giving money only lines the pockets of pimps.

'True,' he laughed. 'The beggars said they wouldn't beg unless they got one rupee per beg. Obviously nobody told them if you're a beggar and you go on strike, you're not going to make a lot of money.'

'A strike?' said Brendon. 'Next thing you'll tell us they need a permit.'

'They do,' said Reece. 'Begging is big business in India, especially if you can get a good spot outside an expensive hotel.'

The bus moved on and the woman cried. We were a long way from home.

Upon arrival at the Taj Bengal Hotel, the Black Craps grabbed a seat in the foyer while John did all the Dad stuff. I felt disoriented, on another planet. A hazy, incense-like fog hovered around us, even though we were indoors. We had intended to have the obligatory beer but no one had the energy. Or the budget, given the prices. So before we knew it, we had retired to our rooms: John and Stew in one, Brendon, Reece and I in the other. After twelve hours on a plane and four hundred pages of *Shantaram*, I was buggered. Couple that with the fact that Reece was the only one who slept in Singapore, and you have a recipe for carnage.

'If you snore tonight, Reece,' Brendon said, 'I'll muzzle you with my pillow.'

'You wouldn't!' laughed Reece.

You never think of India as being cold. Locals know better. Chilly mornings do have one benefit — they mask a variety of smells.

'He would,' I said. 'We didn't sleep one minute last night. It was like a bloody freight train. Seriously, if you sleep with your mouth open I'll pour water down your throat.'

'You wouldn't!' said Reece, now worried.

'Just try it,' finished Brendon before nodding off.

OK, here's where I come clean. When I'm stressed, tired or experiencing a new environment, I have a tendency to sleepwalk — and sleeptalk. It can be embarrassing, but in the last few years at least my episodes have been in the privacy of the marital bed. Normally, if such an occurrence takes place, my wife Amy will say, 'You were standing on the bed at 3 am, trying to stop dinner plates bursting through the wall.'

'So no one was hurt?'

'No, but you got angry when I tried to wake you up.'

And that's the crazy thing about sleepwalking and talking. I am awake, but

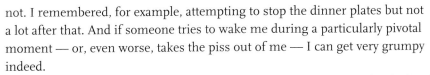

not. I remembered, for example, attempting to stop the dinner plates but not a lot after that. And if someone tries to wake me during a particularly pivotal moment — or, even worse, takes the piss out of me — I can get very grumpy indeed.

Here's all I remember about my first episode in India: standing by the hotel lifts on the fifth floor in nothing but boxer shorts, I awoke, thinking, 'Oh no, I'm sleepwalking.' What I would do, I foolishly thought, was quietly make my way back to the room, inconspicuously fiddle with the air conditioning, and hop back into bed. No one would know any different.

No one would suspect a thing. After all, everyone was asleep and it wasn't as if I'd made any noise.

'Are you okay?' Brendon asked when I entered the room. I could hear Reece sniggering in the dark.

This is where I got a little defensive. They knew something.

'Yeah,' I said, fiddling with the air conditioner. 'Why?'

'Oh, it might have something to do with the fact that you jumped out of bed, yelled, "Stop! Stop! Stop!", opened the door and ran down the hallway.'

'I thought it was my snoring,' said Reece in fits of laughter. 'I thought I'd finally tipped you over the edge and you were about to kill me.'

Brendon, too, was laughing. I climbed into bed, dignity dented. 'Let's not mention this incident at breakfast, OK?' I muttered.

Getting from A to B is a lot easier when 15 million people are yet to wake. In the background, a symbol of Kolkata and something I would have sent home if I had the money: yellow Ambassador taxis.

'Are you kidding?' said Reece. 'This is the only thing we're going to talk about at breakfast!'

Top mates.

True to their word, the Incident was all that was talked about next morning. My room-mates related it in great detail, savouring every word, pausing only for laughs. As Reece scoffed uttapam (an Indian pizza) and stuffed parantha (flatbread), he wondered out loud what would have happened had the door locked behind me. As Brendon ate bacon, eggs and toast, he wondered out loud why he was feeling sick already. As Reece helped himself to more uttapam and puri bhaji — can you see a theme developing here? — he explained how he thought my losing the plot had something to do with his snoring.

'I thought he was about to get up and kill me,' he said.

Yes, the Incident was expertly told and I was expertly embarrassed.

The only people not happy with cricket on Sundays are shepherds, but their accompanying flocks at least save the council mowing the Maidan.

'Can we just go and play some cricket?' I said.

'At least you can't sleepwalk in the day,' said Stew.

'Don't bet on it,' said John.

We had a van and a driver called Khaled. Seeing five tourists must have made his day, but his luck was about to change. Instead of visiting carpet and silk shops, as he politely insisted we should, we informed him we required something far simpler: a tennis ball for backyard cricket. Khaled acquired one for us. Her name was Vicky, and she was what the Indians call a cricket-tennis ball, which is surely an oxymoron.

Khaled's next job was to find a place to play. As we snaked our way through Kolkata — past a silk shop here, a carpet shop there — Reece reminded us why cows are sacred: milk, dung (for building), urine (antiseptic), yoghurt and ghee (clarified butter), while John inquired about India's infamous social cricket matches.

'The huge parks,' he said to Khaled, 'where a million people play at once.'

'Oh, yes, sir!' said Khaled. 'You mean the Maidan. There is one near the next carpet shop!'

'Nice try,' said John, unwrapping Vicky.

The Maidan, as John had imagined, was beyond huge. The largest urban park in Kolkata, and home to hundreds of social Sunday cricket matches, it is often referred to as 'the lungs of Kolkata', and you could see why. In a city that's home to thirteen million people, choked with exhaust fumes, here was an oasis where you could forget your worries and be Tendulkar for the afternoon. That's not to say you could play as of right, as we five 'fresh off the boat' Kiwis imagined. Despite untrimmed outfields, craters the size of golf bunkers, and players wearing what they liked, these matches were eagerly awaited once-a-week events and you couldn't just join in willy-nilly.

And then there were the Maidan's rules, inscribed on a plaque by the main entrance:

No vehicles, bikes or handcarts.
No cooking is allowed.
No cattle, horses, goats, stray dogs.
Anti-social activities are strictly prohibited.
Littering, spitting and other acts of nuisance are prohibited.

In general, except cricket no other games are permitted.

Stew and I wandered past men serving bharer chai — tea in clay pots — feeling like the new kids at school. Everywhere we looked there was cricket, but which game to gatecrash? All we could hear were lost goats, horns and Hindi howzats. In the distance the regal, if incongruous, Victoria Memorial Hall poked her head through a concrete-coloured haze. In the foreground was something far more twenty-first century: a litter of plastic bags and paper.

Eventually we found some players we thought we could give a real run for their money: ten-year-old boys playing under a huge peepul tree. Obviously these guys were too late to get a good place to play or weren't old enough to warrant one, proof being that the tree in question was not, as a traditional ground demands, on the boundary but was rooted right where mid-wicket should have been. Which saved putting a fielder there, I suppose.

'Get to work, Reece,' said John. 'Let's start a match.'

What followed was something we experienced all over India: arguments, despair, shouting, chaos and tears. Reece, scorebook in hand, was swamped with wannabe international cricketers clambering to get their name at the top of the batting order. Brendon and John were accosted by impatient wannabe Bollywood stars who each wanted to catch a glimpse of his mug in digital form. Stew and I, meanwhile, would patiently wait for locals to join the Black Craps. And no one ever wanted to. After all, they didn't want to bowl against us — they wanted to whip our butts.

Reece was doing his best to get some sort of match started. Indian adolescents accosted him as if he was giving out hundred-dollar bills instead of writing down India's batting order. The boys clambered over each other, yelling and swearing in Hindi. As Reece tried to spell their names correctly, each demanded priority.

'I want to open the batting!'

Week-old samosas, stale bread sandwiches and crispy pastry diamonds which have, no doubt, been sitting in the tin trunk since the previous Sunday. Nothing a good dunking in hot sweet chai won't fix!

'Don't choose him, pick me!'

'I want to be captain!'

Reece was slowly being backed into a corner. Given the chance, I'm sure the boys would have written their own names down, but relinquishing control to adolescent, frenzied cricket fanatics with no timetable wouldn't have helped anyone. 'Okay, okay!' he pleaded. 'One at a time! Now, is it Jitesh or Jitash?'

'Jitesh! But I want to be Sehwag!'

'I want to be Sehwag. You can be Ganguly!'

'Ganguly is out of form.'

'That's why you should be him!'

We looked at Reece, who resembled a harassed teacher on a field trip.

'Whoever gave the job of scoring to Blanket Boy is a genius,' I said.

And on it went. Fifteen minutes later and we still hadn't started. Reece, at his wits' end, yelled something in Hindi and the boys swiftly stepped back.

'Handy,' said Brendon. 'Must remember that one.'

I took a seat next to a young boy who was smoking a bidi. Popular throughout India, the small cigarette is a rolled-up leaf with a bit of tobacco enclosed, and tied up with string. Shocked to see such a baby-faced youngster holding one, I asked him his age.

'I'm thirteen,' he said, justifying his fag.

'Isn't that too young to smoke?'

'What do you mean?'

'Thirteen-year-olds don't smoke in India,' I said.

'Two-year-olds smoke in India!' he replied.

I don't know whether smoking really is prevalent among Indian children, but it seems unlikely as it was only recently that international tobacco companies began a major push to the billion potential buyers there. Many different state governments, however, are outlawing smoking, the latest of which is Goa. Many say this will affect business in the foreign tourist season. Or maybe not, given what happened when Delhi's bigwigs banned lighting up in public places. The rule didn't apply to foreigners, who apparently couldn't control their urges the way Indians could. As a result, gloating tourists were allowed to continue to smoke in restaurants, but Indians were not.

Reece eventually gave up writing down names, deciding instead to wing it. 'For Christ's sake, someone just bowl!' he yelled, wrapping his blanket round him like some Jedi Knight. 'The boys say there's only one rule — spin bowling only.'

Stew and I were very happy about this, since we had no pads, gloves or boxes, and we were playing not with Vicky but with a real cricket ball.

The second rule, unbeknown to us, was that the first rule applied only to

Stew as wicketkeeper, not entirely happy that the ball being used is of the real cricket variety. 'Did anyone pack a box?'

JOHN BOUGEN

New Zealand. As we were soon to find out, India were allowed to bowl as fast as they bloody well liked.

T he leaf-covered pitch was like rock. Every time the ball pounded into it, a puff of dirt would hit the air. After India scored a well-rounded twenty-five off four overs, Stew and I asked if we could borrow our opponents' sweaty, junior-sized pads. (I would have worn a box, too, but it was also junior size. It was still in the wrapper, I guess so they could share it.) The kids had written 'India is great' on Reece's scorebook and, judging by two run-outs in our first over (including Stew, who went first ball), I was beginning to believe it.

Enter Utkash. Smaller than his mates — and obviously not highly thought

of, judging by his place in the batting order — Utkash wasn't the best player on the planet. But he was keen, hungry and a nuggety little batting partner. Soon, after squirting twos and fluking singles, we were in reach of the target. I glared down the pitch at a bowler with 'Get lucky with an Irish boy' on his shirt. I had to pinch myself — I was in India, on an Indian pitch, facing an Indian bowler, albeit a ten year old.

With Irish Loverboy imitating Brett Lee, I was more concerned about protecting my manhood than advancing the Black Craps' scorecard. With this in mind, the next time he let one rip I closed my eyes and swung like a madman. To my astonishment, the ball flew off the meat of the bat and rolled past an old army tank by the main road. 'Isn't that a four?' I asked, coming back for the second run.

'No runs!' said Irish Loverboy. 'Anything behind the tree — no runs!'

Ah, the peepul tree. Otherwise known in India as 'The Buddha', this monstrosity of nature ensured that most leg-side shots went no further than your nose, but that was the price you paid for shade.

Utkash hit the winning runs and put on his Man of the Match prize, an Auckland Aces cap. His smile was as wide as the nearby Hoogli River.

'You just play the ones and twos and I'll go for the big shots.' Some inept advice to a batsman who clearly needs new pads for Christmas.

MAIDAN PARK, KOLKATA

INDIA

Sara run out 4
Patan not out 9
Jitesh not out 8
Extras 4

TOTAL 25

BOWLING

Gunn 0-2, Koshal 0-6, Mohit 1-6,
   Utkash 0-12

BLACK CRAPS

Stew run out without facing a ball . 0
Mohit run out 0
Utkash not out 10
Justin not out 13
Extras 3

TOTAL 26

BOWLING

Nitin 0-16, Patan 0-7

BLACK CRAPS TAKE 1-0 LEAD.

Sunday is a big day for the chai
wallah, the tea man working the
Maidan.

TWO

Previous page: Our match outside the Kolkata High Court, viewed from an apartment above the court. These living quarters, centuries old, doubled as a lawyer's office, with files from cases bunched into hundreds of dusty pigeonholes. The occupants were in the middle of breakfast but were more than happy for John to take the shot.

RUNS & RUPEES

lassified advertisement in a Kolkata newspaper: 'HIV groom looking for HIV bride.' Indian morning papers are a treat. Waking in Kolkata, having stayed in bed all night, I was about to read page 401 of *Shantaram,* but asked myself, why read an adventure when you're in the middle of one? Books and movies are pure escapism, meant only for extended plane trips. Once you reach land, you write your own script.

Khaled was waiting for us at reception. As soon as he saw us, he sprang up. 'Carpet shop this morning?' he asked, with the look of a boy on his birthday.

'No, not today,' said Brendon.

'Silk shop?'

'No, we want to go to Eden Gardens, mate,' said Stew.

'But, sir, there is not game on. Pakistan left last week.'

'Doesn't matter. We just want to see it.'

'And then we go to a carpet shop?'

'Maybe,' said Reece.

'Probably not,' said John.

Outside, Kolkata was stretching its arms and getting ready for the day. The horns had started, street vendors were primed and jet-black oversized crows — who seemed to run the joint — dined on every scrap be it newspaper, cigarette packets or leftover peanuts. Overcrowded buses with bars on every window

chugged through gaps, narrowly missing rickshaw drivers, who readily accepted that they were at the bottom of the traffic food chain. The ringing of bicycle bells, blowing of noses (no hanky necessary) and clearing of throats — otherwise known as a dirty old hoik — meant that all was well in India's third-largest city.

Khaled parked by a main intersection. We thanked him and hopped out. 'Carpets later, yes?' he said.

'See how we go,' said Stew.

'Definitely not,' said John.

Two boys, most probably brothers, crept up behind us. The younger one was wearing what looked like a curtain, his brother what could only be described as a large rubbish sack. Their feet were the colour of soot. Like the woman at the lights the previous night, each put his hand to his mouth and grunted. They faked a shiver, but didn't need to. I looked down an alleyway which was still, due to the early morning hour, devoid of people. A man squatted and peed into a shop's roller door.

'Sir,' said the older boy, putting imaginary food in his mouth.

We put our hands in our pockets and turned the other way, pretending to be as hard as nails. Don't give them money. It goes to pimps. It'll just encourage them.

'Here you go,' said Reece, handing them a ten-rupee note. 'Now bugger off.'

The boys accepted with joy. Suddenly we felt mean, stingy, heartless.

'I know you're not supposed to,' said Reece, 'but those poor little guys looked freezing.'

'Oh great, now we feel really bad,' I said.

'Karma, Justin,' he smiled. 'Karma.'

I had never travelled anywhere before with my main focus being finding a game of backyard cricket. Other tourists hunt down museums, monuments or vineyards. We just wanted to roll the arm over.

'We need a bat!' said a purposeful John. 'Has someone got Vicky?'

'Yep,' said Stew, the organised one. 'She'll be dirty in no time, little slut.'

As it was a Sunday, we were having a hard time finding a shop that was open. Sure, there were vendors, but we were after a sports shop with cricket gear.

'Reece, earn your bloody keep and ask Khaled where we can buy a bat.'

Khaled, who was walking behind us, sprang to life when Reece asked in Hindi.

'He reckons we'll find one down the road,' said Reece.

Khaled proudly went to the front of the pack, showing us his city. Within minutes we were walking past street vendors selling cricket bats.

Travellers to India are told their spare change will ultimately end up in the pockets of pimps, but that doesn't stop you feeling bad for not giving anything.

'You want good bat, sir?' one asked.

'Cheap bats, which one do you want?'

Brendon and I stopped to inspect the MRF Tendulkar replicas. 'Please!' said Khaled, grabbing my arm. 'Better price next place.'

The vendor wasn't happy. Khaled didn't care.

We received sinister looks from the remainder of Cricket Bat Alley before Khaled took us into a dark, dingy lane with the roller doors down. With its apparent secrecy and shifty vibe, this was starting to feel more like a drug deal than buying a cricket bat. Every couple of minutes a young boy would be asked to fetch another bat. Another worker, an Indian version of Del Boy from *Only Fools and Horses*, tried to coax us into buying fake Manchester United football shirts.

'No.'

'This one?'

'No.'

'This one?'

'No.'

'David Beckham.'

'Yes, I know.'

'How about this one?'

'No.'

And so on.

John eventually bought a bat named Galaxy, with a horridly girly, purple grip, for four hundred and fifty rupees (eleven US dollars). Khaled seemed stoked. Sadly, this meant a walk of shame back through Cricket Bat Alley. I know it's just business, but it's very difficult carrying the same product past someone who tried to sell it to you ten minutes beforehand. And cricket bats are not the easiest thing to hide in a place like India.

A few years back, I met a Frenchman in an Auckland cafe. His dream, for as long as he could remember, had been to visit Eden Park. It didn't matter that it was midsummer and there wasn't a rugby game on. He just wanted to stand where his heroes had. I had a spare couple of hours, so drove him to Auckland's Home of Rugby. Invariably, as my French friend did, sports fans say the same thing when they see a ground in real life: 'It's a lot smaller than on the TV.'

That, however, is not the case with Kolkata's Eden Gardens. The Home of Cricket (Lord's and the MCG aside), this colossus of a stadium is a 42-inch plasma surround-sound double-woofer of a

Bollywood hopefuls, 'Cricket Bat Alley', Kolkata. They're laughing because they've just found out how much John paid for his bat.

ground. Having been told that you can't just walk in, we just walked in.

Stew and I stood in the main stand having a religious experience. History drenched us. This was the ground where VVS Laxman scored 281 against Australia, with Harbhajan Singh taking a hat trick in the same game. It is a place of pilgrimage, where riots have disrupted matches, entire crowds have been evacuated for being bad sports, and where India stands still to see its national team fry others in a pressure cooker like no other. 'It's a lot smaller than on the TV,' said Stew.

The men in white on the field were employees of a textile company playing a social match — to ninety thousand empty seats. 'Just think, a week ago this place would have been packed,' I said, referring to the rarity of India playing Pakistan at home. Even though the test was drawn, the scores were still proudly displayed on the monster of a scoreboard.

'Not according to the bloke at the gate,' said Brendon. 'They reckon it was only a third full. Combination of high ticket prices, not allowing any food into the stadium, and hideous security checks.'

The facts were hard to fathom since the Pakistan series had been so hotly

anticipated. But if you delved a little deeper, there were other reasons for a poor crowd turnout. Along with the fact that Kolkata was now a working city, unlike the old days when many people had five days to laze around and watch cricket, friction had also been caused by Kolkata's latest curfew. In recent weeks, batons and tear gas had been used to disperse hundreds of protesters, namely local farmers who felt they were being forced to sell their land at cheap rates so the government could replace it with a shipyard and a petrochemical plant. Demonstrators, violent farmers included, had accused the Communist Party of using gangs to try to seize back the district and of killing members of the local farmers' Land Acquisition Resistance Committee who had opposed them. At least thirty-four people had died in the clashes, including six people not long before we arrived in India.

We had seen photos from the massacre before entering Eden Gardens. Displayed for all to see, as family and friends of the victims rallied nearby, were close-ups of bloodied faces and chopped-up bodies. It was shocking and sickening. On the one hand, it was hard to believe that families could post such horrific pictures of their loved ones. On the other hand, if they didn't, among a billion other injustices they simply wouldn't be heard. With such a bulging population and only so much land, there are bound to be complications. But if this really happened, as the farmers claimed, it was an extremely sad piece of Indian history.

Eden Gardens, Kolkata – capacity ninety thousand – shown with about as big a crowd as the Black Craps would pull if they played in the Indian Premier League (IPL).

The welcome silence of an empty stadium was a distant memory by the time we stepped back out onto Eden Garden Road. And the six-month-old baby by itself on the footpath served as a reminder of where we were. Brendon and I were stunned. We looked around for a parent. OK, so the baby was happily asleep, with an empty bottle resting on her chin, but there was no parent in sight and she was only a few metres from the fumes and chaos. Judging by the way the other guys marched on, the sight of an abandoned child had more of an effect on the new dads in the group. (Note to helicopter parents: kids are bloody hardy.)

Khaled had told Reece that he thought the High Court would be a great place to play.

'Of course, why didn't we think of that?' I asked.

'As long as we don't get arrested,' said Stew. 'I don't want to go to an Indian jail.'

But before we could get back in the van, four teenage boys halted our progress. 'How much did you pay for your bat?' one asked.

'I don't know,' said John. 'Four hundred?'

'Four fifty,' said Brendon.

'Four fifty!' the other laughed.

'One eighty,' he said, holding up the identical bat.

John, never one to enjoy being ripped off, looked down at the boy's hunk of willow. 'One eighty, you reckon?' he asked, reaching in his pocket.

'Don't be stupid, John,' I said. 'How many bats do we need?'

As a result of his excessive amount of travelling, particularly in the last few years on the All Nations Quest, John had developed an enviable approach to touts. He was very generous to the good ones but didn't suffer fools. Where other travellers are polite, even to idiots, John's unique 'Fuggoff!' was the perfect way either to deny or confuse, all in a way that sounded like, if there is such a thing, a lovely rejection.

'What's your good name?'

'Fuggoff!'

'Please come into my shop.'

'Fuggoff!'

'No buy, just look. Looking is free.'

'Fuggoff!'

'You paid too much for that bat.'

'Fuggoff. Did I?'

Us: 'He's not buying another one.'

We took Khaled's advice — as if we had other plans — and a short time later pulled up to the Kolkata High Court. The oldest of its kind in India, it was established in 1862 and has jurisdiction over the state of West Bengal and the Union Territory of the Andaman and Nicobar Islands (two island groups near Myanmar and Indonesia). Behind the picture-postcard frontage of the building is an alley flanked by run-down, three-storey apartment blocks. Judging by the condition of the flats, this was not where judges lived but rather clerks and junior staff of the High Court.

It was Sunday, a day of rest. Men bathed and drank tea. And when I say bathe, I don't mean a quick shit, shower and shave. These naturists scrubbed their backs as if they were decks that had been pounded by the ills of winter. Naked but for loincloths, they were rigorous, thorough, and sometimes downright aggressive. They relished every stroke, ringing every last sud out of their ever-decreasing soaps. Saving water was clearly not an issue either, with a nearby pump gushing more than could be used.

Virtually every Indian, even those dossing down on the streets, will find a way to have a full body wash every day. Sunday means there's more time to take things at a leisurely pace.

Khaled settled on a park in front of where some adolescents were playing street cricket. They sprinted to the van, no doubt thinking we were celebrities. The fact that we weren't didn't seem to disappoint. Reece grabbed his blanket, Brendon his camera, and the rest of us hopefully some kind of form with the bat.

When Stew and I started bowling, locals stopped and laughed. They peered out of their apartment windows. A shop vendor lit a cigarette and put his feet up. Old men listened to their transistor radios. When official cars carrying official people drove through, we let them pass. And when Stew's practice shots flew over the High Court's iron gates, kids squeezed through and retrieved them. We tried to pass the bat to the kids, but they didn't want a bar of it. They just wanted to bowl at us, and lined up for the chance.

'Shall we use Vicky?' I asked, pulling her out of the team bag.

'No way,' said Stew, pointing to the windows.

'This is the High Court, remember?' said Reece, while the kids glued themselves to his scorebook.

The pitch was hard and even, with a brilliantly consistent bounce. (But I guess that's what you'd expect from a road.) We won the toss and batted. As Stew had pointed out, there was a plethora of windows in the general vicinity, so I tried my best not to hit the ball too hard. As it turned out I needn't have worried, as I had contracted Stew's 'Run Out First Ball' disease.

'Yes!'

'No!'

'Wait!'

'You go!'

'No, you go!'

'Wait, I said!'

Them: 'Yay!'

'Shit, sorry.'

The Black Craps put on a solid twenty-eight, and the India Under-Nines

Left: This cover drive may look impressive, but it pays to remember I didn't score a single run in the real game. But what a practice shot!

Above: A brilliant bunch of kids and a game we'll long remember. What impressed us most was their total lack of respect for judges!

appeared to be in no trouble at all. These boys could bat. Left-handers resembling Yuvraj Singh tucked deliveries down to third man for one. Right-handers the spitting image of Mahendra Singh Dhoni smashed balls over mid-wicket, calypso-style, onto apartment balconies. Old men playing backgammon ducked for cover. Mothers hanging out washing evaded tennis-ball rockets with consummate ease, as if they had done it all before. And Stew and I were left to chase balls that due to the very nature of the outfield — smooth, solid concrete — rolled merrily to the other end of the High Court.

The India Under-Nines had victory in their sights, until I brought out my secret weapon. (OK, truth be told, the only bloke who hadn't bowled.) Stew gave his sunhat to the umpire and came in to bowl the final over. We needed one wicket; they needed two runs. Pace and accuracy combined to see Stew's first ball rifle into the makeshift wickets — a judges' parking sign.

We celebrated.

'No wicket!' the kids yelped. 'Didn't bounce!'

This was obviously a local rule, and one which we had to abide by if we were to stay friends with this bunch. With a single run needed from the final ball, Stew went to the top of his run-up (about three steps) and came in to bowl.

Black Craps: rubbish. India: great. Reece: glad someone else is doing the scoring.

Then the sound of tin, another wicket, and we had won the game.

Stew was humble and gracious in victory. 'We were unbeatable! We were on fire! We are the Black Craps!'

'Stew,' I said, 'they were nine.'

HIGH COURT, KOLKATA

BLACK CRAPS

Justin run out 0
Kishor not out 10
Raju caught by Dilip, bowled Babul . 4
Sonu hit government vehicle 0
Extras 14

TOTAL 28

BOWLING

Monu 0-7, Babul 1-3, Rajesh 0-4,
  Dilip 0-5

INDIA

Monu run out 2
Babul run out 3
Bipin caught Stew, bowled Justin . . 4
Rajesh bowled Kishor 2
Dililp bowled Steve 5
Extras 13

TOTAL 29

MAN OF THE MATCH

Kishor, who wore his new Auckland Aces
  cap with pride

NEW ZEALAND WON BY ONE RUN
TO LEAD THE SERIES 2–0.

After the obligatory high fives, backslapping and autographs (it's tough being a touring side), we jumped in the van and set off to eat. Having been in Kolkata for only a few meals, this was always a slightly apprehensive time because what goes in your mouth in the next hour determines how well your next few days will go.

'When I was a tour guide,' said Reece, 'I used to know how a group would be from how soon they started talking about their bowel motions.'

'What do you mean?' asked Brendon, a little squeamishly.

'Well, if we sat down to breakfast on the first morning and someone said, "I'm too scared to fart", and the next said, "I'm already on the blockers", I knew they'd be a cruisy group. Alternatively, if everyone avoided the subject altogether I knew I'd be spending two weeks with a humourless bunch of gonzos.'

'Stop the van!' said Brendon. 'I think I need to go!'

'That's the spirit,' said Reece. 'This is a good group.'

'No, seriously,' wheezed Brendon. 'Stop the van. I need to go!'

Khaled gave a wry smile and pulled into a five-star hotel. Brendon disembarked and walked gingerly through reception to the magic signs.

'Don't you want a newspaper?' I asked. But he was gone.

Brendon returned to a barrage of abuse which, due to his inner rumblings, he couldn't rebut. We knew Delhi Belly would reach us all at some time, probably sooner rather than later, but when it wasn't us, we had to make the most of it.

We continued through Kolkata's streets and lanes. The horns continued, as did the familiar 'Cor! Cor!' of crows, overshadowed only by the screeching of a nearby bus's brakes. We marvelled at the face of Kolkata: the yellow Ambassador. Otherwise known as the Morris Oxford, this piece of history on wheels is from a time gone by, straight from your granddad's garage. And its horn means business. Deep and resonant, it resembles a classic tune from a 78 on a wind-up gramophone rather than the stripped-down, ringtone-styled horn on a modern vehicle.

Love thy neighbour; flog power from thy neighbour. In many cities power theft is considered a national right.

Typically, on each of these eye-popping jaunts around the city, we'd see some poor bugger on a push bike, minding his own business, utterly oblivious and out of harm's way, getting a rocket up the arse in the form of a bus horn at full volume. Unbelievably, the rider in question wouldn't, as would be the case in most 'civilised' countries, give a stern middle finger, but would instead accept his fate and move over obligingly. We saw this time and again, and it never ceased to make us smile.

Eating lamb curry for lunch — even Brendon — we were reminded of a sticker we'd seen on our taxi van in Singapore: wonderful bright photos of parrots, kittens, puppies, sheep and roosters, with the slogan, 'Love us, don't eat us.'

'Do you believe that, do you?' Stew asked the driver.

'Sorry, sir?' said the driver, tuning into Stew's conversation.

'That sticker with the animals, is that part of your belief?'

'Yes, sir,' he said. 'I don't eat meat.'

We all looked at the sticker again.

'I eat meat,' I said. 'But I don't think I'd eat most of what's on that sticker.'

'Oh, come on,' said Brendon. 'That macaw looks pretty tasty.'

'And don't knock kitten till you've tried it,' said Reece.

'What about you?' said the driver, looking in the rear-vision mirror. 'Are you a vegetarian?'

'We're from New Zealand,' said John.

'Oh,' said the driver.

'And we're sheep farmers,' chimed in Stew.

THREE

Previous page: Game three, The Cow Paddock, Siliguri. Not entirely sure what
Stew's up to. We know he misses his animals, but even so . . .

ivea puts back into your skin what the city takes out.' The billboard we saw as we left Kolkata said it all. As our van made its way to the airport, we all felt a twinge of excitement, knowing we'd be in Darjeeling, in the far north-east of the country, by sunset. But first we had a van ride, a plane ride and yet another van ride, which we were told would take three hours to cover sixty kilometres.

'That's got to be bullshit,' I said to Stew.

'I reckon as well.'

In the newspapers, cricket was everywhere. Ganguly had scored a double ton against the Pakistanis, and every Indian we spoke to was salivating at the prospect of the forthcoming tour of Australia. In *The Telegraph* was a tragic tale of a boy who had lost his left arm and leg trying to retrieve a tennis ball in a game of street cricket. Fourteen-year-old Shivranshu Chhuneja used to be the most popular boy in school. Now his friends were 'too scared to look at him' and his right thumb was the only workable part of his limbs. He had been playing cricket with his friends when somebody smacked the ball over a wall. When Shivranshu jumped over, eleven thousand volts gripped his body. 'He was burning like a candle,' said his distraught mother. 'He could not make a sound, not even shout for help. Then he just fell off, virtually smouldering.'

Our first flight in India, to Bagdogra, was successful and uneventful apart from the curry, which was so hot you needed gloves. As we now had a small collection of bats, we needed somewhere to put them. Taping them to the outsides of our bags became the only option, although some Black Craps doubted they would arrive with us later in the day. There were four bats in all, on three bags.

'Fifty rupees says they don't all make it to Bagdogra,' said John.

'No one will steal them,' I said as the last one, the horrid, girly Galaxy with the purple handle, was being strapped to my backpack. 'Fifty rupees says they don't.'

Travel calculator: two dollars. OK, can proceed.

'Indians respect cricket,' I said.

'Fifty rupees.'

And we shook hands.

'How much did you pay for that bat again?' I asked.

'Four hundred and fifty,' said John.

'Could have got it for a hundred and eighty.'

'Fifty rupees,' reinforced John.

The flight was short, only an hour, and we soon arrived in the 'B' place. (Every country has its city whose name you forget; Bagdogra was ours.) As we waited for the bags to arrive, I started to doubt India and its people. Maybe the bats would be stolen. Maybe John, with all his travel and 'Fuggoffs', was right. After all, packing them like that was a pretty dumb thing to do.

When they arrived safe and sound, all four of them, I felt proud. 'I never doubted India and its people,' I said. 'I knew they wouldn't be stolen.'

'Yeah right,' said Brendon.

'Where's John?' I asked. 'I want my money.'

Then, in the distance, we heard a barely decipherable but clearly audible rant. 'What the fuck's wrong with this country? You used to be able to smoke where you liked! Honestly, this place has gone to the pack! Rack and ruin! Hell in a handcart!'

'He's over there,' said Brendon.

The rest of us were comforted to hear what was becoming a typical outburst from John. The fact that India was mirroring the rest of the smoke-free, PC world was just too much for him to take. Plus, he reasoned, the Indians could handle it. 'They like a bit of gyp. Being polite isn't really an option.'

A hell of a way to make a living. Families in Siliguri work all day crushing river rocks, to be picked up by trucks and sold for road and building construction.

Indeed, so far on the trip, John had taken great pleasure in doing as he'd always done when visiting India: bartering down to absolute base price, then tipping like crazy.

India demanded you had your wits about you. 'I was having a fag just before we left Kolkata,' he said, passing me my fifty rupees. 'There was a group of sixty or so Americans sitting next to me. They asked their tour guide where the shopping hot spots were. He proceeded to tell them all the places he would get a kickback. I sat there thinking, should I tell them it's all bullshit? No, fuck it, they're Americans.'

First-timers do it hard in India.

Kabir, our new guide, was waiting outside the terminal. An instantly likeable guy, if a little uptight, he had greased-down hair with a part in the middle. His English was spot-on, and he gave each of us a mala — a lei made from marigolds, a traditional offering made on religious occasions or as a presentation to honoured guests. Saffron, the colour of marigolds, is Hinduism's most auspicious colour. More importantly, it made us feel as though we were in Fiji.

After the chaos of Kolkata, the air in the 'B' place seemed clean. There was room to move. There seemed to be less noise. And soon we would be on Highway 55, bound north for a place fondly known as the Queen of the Hills. But not before we passed bizarre billboards: 'Cafe cum bar', 'Flame throwing bartenders', 'Hot DJs and a hotel goat'.

About half an hour into the trip we passed through the city of Siliguri and crossed a bridge over a riverbed. For as far as the eye could see, Indians were excavating and breaking rock with little more than prehistoric-looking tools. Later, we were told, a truck would turn up and take their efforts away to be sold. We got out of the van and listened to the donk, donk, donk of metal on rock. It went for miles. Whole families had set up camp, chiselling what ultimately became sizeable mounds of fine shingle, resembling a concrete version of Hobbiton in *The Lord of the Rings*. Watching tired, weathered-looking women, bent over, knee-deep in water, hammering rocks loose from larger ones made us, not the first time, feel that fate plays a huge part in where you are born.

Further down the road there was much excitement as we spied a game of cricket being played on a barren field. (As the tour was still in its infancy, seeing a game of cricket was — we thought, anyway — akin to spotting a white rhino in Gibraltar. Later, it would be as common as seeing Brendon sprint, stiff-legged, to the gents.) Kabir resembled the confused-looking guide we had left behind in Kolkata. 'You want to stop here?' he asked. 'Why?'

'When's the last time you played cricket?' John asked.

'I haven't played since I was in school,' replied Kabir.

'Well, that's about to change!' we said, exiting the van.

The boys in the middle looked as puzzled at our arrival as Kabir. I guess it did look pretty strange, five wide-eyed Kiwis traversing India in a mobile goldfish bowl. Reece grabbed his blanket and scorebook. He didn't need to be asked anymore. He knew his job. Brendon and John sprang out to take some pictures while Stew and I prepared for arguments.

The pitch was as hard as ice, a solitary piece of barren, bumpy dirt in the middle of a cow paddock. Even Tony Greig would have had trouble slicing his keys into this sucker. Although, full credit to the groundsman — when you tapped the strip with your bat, it sounded like a real pitch from a game on TV. Like any backyard wicket it had its quirks, namely gaping holes and unpredictable, dangerous mounds, but other than that it was a fast, grassless piece of Indian turf.

As cows glared and geese fled, Stew and I approached the apprehensive kids.

'You want a game?' I asked, mimicking a leg spinner.

Aliens, they thought. One bald. One wearing a blanket. Two with movie cameras. And one with eyebrows so big you could knit a jumper out of them.

'Cricket!' reinforced Stew, swinging the Galaxy. 'You want to play?'

More blank looks. Reece asked the same question in Hindi. The boy with the

India was tracking towards the elimination of polio, but the superstitious belief that vaccination is the government's way of sterilising children has dented progress somewhat. A single shot would have meant Samson could have been bowling and not keeping wicket.

bat marched over to the stumps and started pulling them out.

'What's he doing?' I asked. 'Don't they want to play?'

Reece translated. The boy replied.

'Ah,' said Reece. 'He says this is their number-two ground. They want to play you on their number-one ground.'

One thing we had started to do in India, almost unintentionally, was mimic the Indian accent. Unlike us, Reece did it for a reason: 'It's easier to be understood if you put on an accent.'

'Even if it makes you sound Welsh?' asked John.

'Yes.'

'Or Irish?' asked Brendon.

'Yes.'

'Or like a complete spanner?' I added.

'Not hard for you,' said Reece.

And he was right. Even though many Indians spoke English, many couldn't understand our bastardisation of it. They spoke fast, like us. We were speaking the same language, but no one knew it. Sometimes it took a good five minutes before both parties heard words they understood. If we ever did have any trouble, as was the case with the boy moving his troops to the number-one ground, we'd yell, 'Reece, get your arse over here! Can't understand a word this joker's saying!'

'Reece,' yelled Stew. 'Get your arse over here!'

We had moved to the number-one ground, a fifty-metre walk uphill from the number-two ground. These boys were surely the only backyard players on the planet with home and away venues. Not only that, the pitch we were standing on was absolutely identical to the one we had just shifted from.

'What do you want?' said Reece, trying to write down some sort of batting order.

'Tell them to pick a captain.'

'You tell them to pick a captain. I'm busy.'

Clearly Reece was still flustered by his nemesis, the scorebook. You had to feel for him. Three days ago he'd never so much as seen one. Now he had to know the difference between leg byes, wides, sundries and dead balls. Actually, screw him — he was getting a free trip.

I attempted to take the initiative, putting on an Indian accent worse than Peter Sellers', and asked our new mates to name a captain.

'You sound Welsh,' said John.

Incredibly, the accent worked wonders. The boys gathered around and the boy holding the bat pointed to his mates. Then someone yelled. Within a minute or so, a bike carrying three more boys turned up. They all pointed to a lanky one with an infectious smile, sitting on the carrier.

'This is your captain?' I asked.

'Yes,' they laughed. 'Samson.'

They continued cracking up, but the joke was on us. As the first two boys got off the bike, Samson literally fell off, landing on his hands. He crossed his flaccid, floppy legs, and looked at us as if we had the problem.

'Our captain!' the others squealed with delight.

We didn't know where to look. Was this funny? Were we allowed to laugh?

'Samson!' they yelped. 'Our captain!'

Samson walked on his hands to the wicket-keeping position and got ready for the first ball. There was no sympathy or pity. After the initial prank, no one referred to it again. It made us wonder whether this wasn't the first time they had used their polio-victim friend to get a cheap laugh. If it was a regular occurrence, Samson showed no signs of bitterness. I guess in India, like anywhere, you make do with what you've got.

We lost the toss. It was decided that the game would be seven players a side, each facing three balls. By the time we batted, after a lengthy twenty balls, Stew was adamant that the pitch had dried out. 'Good toss to win, I reckon,' he said.

We were on a paltry seventeen, needing to double that off the last ball to win.

'No pressure,' Brendon said, as Stew took guard.

'Yeah right,' he said, hitting what looked to be a definite six before holing out to a brilliant catch just short of the boundary, where cows were happily grazing. It was Ganguly, the batsman who had peppered the boundary himself while batting.

Samson was given the cap as Man of the Match. At first, I was worried that this might have highlighted his disadvantage or showed unhealthy favouritism. Memories of a forty-eight-hour train ride when I backpacked across Tanzania came flooding back. Having broken down in the middle of nowhere, and this being Africa (i.e. no one was in a hurry to move), we were swamped by a bunch of kids from a nearby village. Judging by the way they were staring, they had never seen the likes of us before. Then a German man next to me did something I'll never forget. He picked out a disfigured boy from the back and physically pushed the other kids aside to get to him. 'Not you!' he said, pushing one kid away. 'Not you!' he barked, clambering past another. He finally reached the boy — whose injuries could only have been caused by a dreadful fire — handed him a soft toy, then got back on the train. I don't know how this story ended, as the train was soon on its way, but the others kids' vitriolic resentment was clear. It was fine for the German; he had a beer, a nice camera and a future. The burns victim had a soft toy and another reason to be victimised by his fellows.

Samson, I reasoned, was different — as were all of the cricketers we gave gifts to. We weren't giving money; we were rewarding them for whipping our butts on the cricket pitch. Even better, they never expected anything and were genuinely surprised when we pulled a cap from our bags as a record for their talent.

India and the Black Craps shook hands and huddled for a hurried team photo. Kabir was getting restless; we had a mountain to drive up. You could tell what he was thinking: most tourists don't stop for a backyard cricket match on the first cow paddock they see. Samson adjusted his hat for the picture and smiled alongside his good, decent mates.

THE COW PADDOCK, SILIGURI

INDIA

Lahul don't know how out, Reece never
wrote it down **3**
Ravinder don't know how out, Reece
got confused **1**
Taposh don't know how out, Reece was
flustered **2**
Sarfraj don't know how out, Reece's pen
ran out **5**
Ganguly don't know how out, Reece
told us to fuck up **7**
Diraj don't know how out, Reece asked
what a no-ball was **4**
Chanan don't know how out, Reece
asked why he had to score **6**
Extras **5**

TOTAL 33

BOWLING

Dilip 1-5, Santosh 0-2, Suraj 0-9, Kabir
0-5, Stew 0-4, Justin 0-4

BLACK CRAPS

Vijay 'How many runs for a wide?' . . **4**
Dilip 'Was that a leg bye?' **3**
Santosh 'Well, if you don't tell
me, I don't fucking know!' **0**
Suraj 'Who caught that?' **1**
Kabir 'Hasn't he already batted?' . . **5**
Justin 'Do we have to write down
the score?' **4**
Stew 'This is supposed to be
a holiday!' **0**
Extras **6**

TOTAL 23

BOWLING

Lahul 0-4, Ravinder 0-2, Taposh 0-2,
Safraj 0-5, Ganguli 0-3, Diraj 0-5,
Chanan 0-0

INDIA WINS.
BLACK CRAPS LEAD THE SERIES 2–1.

ith our first loss in the bag, we hit the road. The corners were as blind as most of the drivers. I guess that's why signs, a few kilometres apart, littered the roadside:

Take it easy on the ride, don't be suicide.
Donate your blood to the bank, not to the road.
Caress my curves gently.
Kindness is giving the right of way.
Take it slowly in life — don't speed to eternity.
Life is a gift from God — save it.

The terrain changed quickly. Gone were the dusty, billboard-laden main roads advertising Pepsi, soap and cellphones. Tea plantations and jungle, complete with wires running along the edge to keep out wild elephants (they eat farmers' crops, especially rice), were a welcome change. But progress was slow. Highway 55, the road to Darjeeling, runs beside a railway line. It's a tight affair, at its widest barely allowing two vehicles to pass. Smoky old vehicles chugged up steep inclines, often changing to first or second gear to get a good run-up. The blind corners forced drivers to use their horns.

Meanwhile, Reece's abilities with the scorebook were coming under fire. 'You seem to be having a bit of trouble with this thing,' said Stew, analysing the day's match stats as we rumbled round another blind bend.

'It's bloody impossible!' said Reece.

'One of these overs only has six balls.'

'That's what you told me,' said Reece. 'Six balls to an over.'

'Not if you bowl a no-ball.'

'You get an extra ball for a no-ball,' said Brendon, sensing this was going to be fun. 'And another run.'

'What about a wide?'

'Same,' said Stew. 'You haven't even written down how he was out. Or who got him out. And you don't put runs and bowling figures in the same column.'

'Ah, Jesus!' said Reece. 'Why don't you do it then?'

'I can't score and play,' said Stew.

'It's not easy, Blanket Boy,' I said. 'But you did an admirable job in Kolkata.'

'That's because John was helping me!'

'How much further, Kabir?' John asked our guide, putting an unlit fag in his mouth. The 'Darjeeling' sign said fifty-eight kilometres.

'Three hours,' said Kabir.

'That's got to be bullshit,' I said to Stew.

'I reckon too,' Stew said, with a certain amount of apprehension.

During the British Raj, Darjeeling's temperate climate attracted residents escaping the heat of the plains during the summer. Kabir's mother for many years had done the same. Darjeeling produces about a quarter of India's tea. And its toy train (operational since 1881) is listed as a World Heritage site, and is one of the few hill railways still operating in India.

While these were all interesting facts Kabir was regaling us with, they didn't get us up the hill any faster. We were now going at a crawl, trailing every other decrepit vehicle attempting to reach the clouds. We snaked, squeezed, stopped and started. And John was starting to get pretty bloody snotty. He even faked needing to take a leak, just so he could jump out and have a cigarette. We played my four-year-old daughter's yellow ukulele. We told dirty jokes. I tried to read page 504 of *Shantaram* but quickly felt carsick. Brendon puckered his butt cheeks. John fiddled with his cigarette packet. As we inched up the mountain, we started to believe what we had been told back in the 'B' place: sixty kilometres equals three hours.

It feels wrong not to enjoy every moment of travel. You think that every minute, every mile, every meal should be unforgettable. But sometimes it's just long and tedious. Every corner looks the same. Change down a gear. Beep the horn. Change up a gear. Beep the horn. How do these drivers do it? Wonder what my family are doing. Hungry. Thirsty. Sign in distance. Desperately want it to be 'Darjeeling eight kilometres'. It's getting closer. I think I can make out what it says. A hot meal and a beer must be only minutes away! Maybe even a shower . . .

'How much further, Kabir?' John asked.

'Two hours,' Kabir smiled. 'We should be there by dark.'

'I believe him now,' I said to Stew.

'Me too,' he replied.

The best thing to think about was nothing at all. With that in mind, we finally approached civilisation. It was the road into Darjeeling, and it looked just like a movie set, as if a scene from a children's story had been transported to the Himalayas. Precariously perched on unbelievably abrupt cliffs, each dwelling was made of clay, with tree hut-sized wooden balconies. Oil lamps aided the dwindling light. Many homes were also shops, their proud owners giving toothless smiles to the gormless cricketers in the Mobile Goldfish Bowl.

Playing backyard cricket held its own challenges in Darjeeling. First we had to find a backyard!

Despite the cold, a few front doors were open, leaving an unobstructed view through lounges straight out to Mount Kangchenjunga, towering over an azure sky.

The rose-tinted glasses we wore, however, weren't shared by the Himalayan locals, who were busy going about their afternoon schedules. Men ambled forlornly, hunched over under the weight of potato sacks. Black exhaust fumes choked open-air stalls. School kids walked home, arm in arm, more for warmth than out of kinship. And still the horns — always the horns! Even at the foothills of the mighty Himalayas, impatient, road rage-filled drivers were desperate to get home.

Kabir must have read our minds as we passed over another terrifying drop. 'In the monsoon season, some houses have been known to fall off,' he said.

We peered over the edge and felt ill.

'A few years ago an entire family fell from these cliffs. They all died.'

'Don't they move away to try and protect themselves?' I asked.

'No, they go down with their property.'

FOUR

Previous page: 'Mine!' Indecision in Darjeeling.

A GOOD CUPPA CHAR

The Windermere Hotel on Darjeeling's Observatory Hill is straight out of a Jane Austen novel. Established in the nineteenth century as a boarding house for bachelor English and Scottish tea planters, it was converted into a hotel just before the outbreak of World War II. It is extravagant and over the top in a post-colonial, 'let's pretend it's still the Raj era' kind of way. Porters, resplendent in morning suits and white gloves, helped unload our grimy backpacks from the Goldfish Bowl. They escorted us to reception, where a woman, similarly dressed, spoke with the proverbial plum in her mouth. It was all terribly British. Maybe it was the cold, or the altitude. Whatever it was, within minutes we were all bent over laughing.

There was a bell sitting on the counter. I couldn't resist. Ding! 'Manuel!'

The *Fawlty Towers* reference was lost on the receptionist, but not on the Black Craps. Aside from the view of the Himalayas, this hotel wouldn't have been out of place next to Basil's Torquay residence. Once the laughter had died down and we had passed over our passports, we were shown to our rooms. John and Stew shared theirs, which had an open fire and a painting of Darjeeling's own Tenzing Norgay. Another porter was stacking wood and coal.

'What, what!' said Stew.

'What, what, indeed!' we replied.

'Shall we have a quick bath then meet for a sherry before dinner, chaps?'

'Right you are!' we said. 'Toodle pip!'

Some rooms at the Windermere — complete with creaky floorboards and peach-coloured curtains — had the smell of a rest home. Others housed obscure relics from a time gone by. This wasn't a hotel; it was a museum, a time warp, a lost world of grace and elegance not fit for five bumbling Black Craps.

Our porter took us to our sleeping quarters. Once there, we looked at the lonely double bed in the corner of the room. An uncomfortable laugh came from three men not happy with the way their evening was shaping up.

Reece scratched his head, searching for the right words. 'Small problem, gee [a term of endearment in Hindi],' he said. 'We are three.'

'No problem,' said the porter, pointing to the double bed.

'Yes, big problem!' said Brendon. 'One of us snores, and the other's a sleepwalker.'

'I told you,' I said, 'I only do that sort of thing every couple of months.'

'Yeah right,' said Brendon.

Reece had to convince the porter, who was still stoking the fire with fresh coal, that the room really was unsuitable. This might be a boys'-own trip, but sleeping three to a bed, spoons-style, sent shivers down our spines.

'Gee!' he stressed. 'Quite seriously, we are three. We need three beds.'

'You don't have to sleep touching,' said the porter, uninterested.

Reece earned his keep. The porter was soon fixing us a new room.

We arrived in the dining room to more *Fawlty Towers* quotes from Stew. 'Papers arrived yet, Fawlty?' he asked.

'Not yet, Major,' I replied.

We sat where we would be seated for every meal. There didn't seem to be anyone else staying. Maybe it was too cold. It certainly was hard to believe that a few hours ago we had been playing cricket in short sleeves. As Edith Piaf played on the stereo, we wondered who had vomited on the wallpaper. We drank an Indian white wine that tasted as though it had come straight from the drains of Kolkata. But the meal, when we weren't laughing our butts off due to the altitude, was superb:

Ginger & Carrot Soup
Roast Chicken with Roasted Potatoes *or* Tandoori Roti
Seasonal Vegetables

Rajmah

Kashmiri Pulao

Fish Tikka

Palak Paneer

Papad, Achar and Chutney

Steamed Jam Pudding with Hot Custard

Coffee from Baba Budan Hills or Tea from Darjeeling

Observatory Hill, Darjeeling. We woke at 5 am in the hope of catching a glimpse of Tibet, Bhutan and Nepal, as well as twenty of the highest mountain peaks of the world. But it was cloudy.

It was a set menu and the food just kept coming. No doubt about it, sitting down to eat, particularly at breakfast time, was fast becoming the highlight of the trip. At home, with families and schedules, we often eat on the run or not at all. To take your time, crack jokes and have nowhere to be (apart from on a cow paddock or in an alleyway) was a luxury no one was taking for granted.

As the bottle of Indian white neared its end — and those of us drinking it reached for a bucket — John asked Brendon why he didn't drink. 'Not saying you have to,' he said, 'I was just wondering. Is it a choice thing?'

'Heavily allergic to it,' said Brendon, slurping a Coke. 'Had a beer when I was in my teens. Made me really sick. Can't stomach any alcohol at all.'

'That's probably a good thing considering this wine,' I said.

'Second that,' said Stew.

The greatest hits of Edith Piaf continued. Our waiter, who still had not so much as a scuff on his immaculate suit nor a speck of dirt on his glistening white gloves, asked if we'd like a hot drink.

'Coffee for me,' said John, patting his stomach.

'Coffee?' said Brendon. 'This is Darjeeling!'

'I don't care. I'm having coffee.'

'It's the home of tea!' I said.

'I want coffee!'

'Darjeeling tea!' said Reece.

'And can I smoke?' John asked the waiter, ignoring us.

'No, sir,' he smiled. 'No smoking.'

'Jesus Christ,' John muttered. 'Rack and ruin, this country, I tell you.'

At its best, life is full of surprises: having a party you knew nothing about; discovering someone else has paid for your parking ticket; watching your room-mate run down a hotel hallway in Kolkata, yelling, 'Stop, stop, stop!' But nothing, absolutely nothing on earth compares to jumping into bed in the Himalayas and finding a hottie in your bed.

'Oooh!' said Reece, wriggling under his covers. 'I haven't had one of these since I was a kid!'

He promised that he would be the last to fall asleep so Brendon and I could nod off before the snoring started. It didn't matter; we all slept the sleep of babies under duvets the weight of a yak's coat.

Any flat piece of land in Darjeeling will always be well used. Black Craps vs. India, Gorkha Stadium.

The next morning, as a bone-chilling wind outside whipped off some of the planet's highest peaks, we sat at the same table, were served by the same waiter, looked at the same vomit-coloured walls, and John had more coffee in the home of tea.

Darjeeling is world-famous for its cuppa char. There are three different types of tea: the 'first first', 'second first' and 'third first'. The 'first first' is a light, fruity tea, which is generally the first of the tea leaves to be harvested for that season (around March). The 'second first' is the second harvest, which usually occurs in late spring or early summer. These leaves have had all the time in the world to mature, and their flavour is strong and fully grown. The colour of the brew is a lot darker, too. Finally, the 'third first' is a tea not as prized as the other two, but if it were to be compared would probably be more like the 'first first' than the 'second first.' Given the option, my first choice would be the 'second

first', as it's generally less acidic than the rest. On the other hand, the 'first first' and the 'third first' could be the first choice for those who don't like their cuppa char too strong.

Confused? Just have coffee like John.

At the gentlemanly hour of 9.30 am, our driver arrived and asked about our day's plans. 'We want to find a game of cricket, gee,' said Reece.

Once again, a look of dejection from the driver. His shoulders slumped as he slipped the van into first. You could see what he was thinking: why do I get the Kiwi backyard-cricket freaks who wouldn't know a Kashmir from a pashmina?

Much to our guide's anguish, we soon found ourselves parked outside Gorkha Stadium. A derelict, empty coliseum of sorts, the once-proud arena looked as if its builders had left after Friday drinks and never returned. We were told it was a major venue for big tournaments, exhibitions and cultural activities. To us, it looked like a stadium the Taliban might run.

The view was daunting; the sand beneath our feet Waikiki-white. Prayer flags wrestled the wind, draped between sky-high Himalayan pines. Impossibly balanced homes perched on the hill, stealing a view of a pitch most groundskeepers would die for. As for the rest of the stadium, anywhere else in the world it would have been pulled

down, but it still had charm and, though it had clearly seen better days, a certain amount of history. This seemed typical in India: a once-regal, refined and revered monument now needed too much dough for upkeep. For some unknown reason — I guess because Darjeeling was so stunningly beautiful — it gave the false impression that its people weren't poor. How, one could argue, could you have no money yet have an unobstructed view of the world's third-highest mountain, Kanchenjunga? But Darjeeling's people, like most in India, lived hand-to-mouth, many having no access to a toilet or clean running water.

As no one in Kolkata thought we had any show of playing cricket in the Himalayas because of the temperature, we felt quietly vindicated when we found some teenage boys bashing a ball around by the stadium's far goalposts. We walked over to them. They didn't appear too keen to play a team of plonkers wearing knitted cricket vests. The young ones laughed at Stew's hairless head when he took his cap off. 'Baldy!' they screamed. Stew took it well. I thought they were walking a fine line, since he was carrying a cricket bat.

As usual, we acquired the squirts and India selected a team worthy of playing in the Indian Premier League. John, seeing the imbalance in power, abandoned his camera and demanded a call-up. Brendon headed for the hills to get some once-in-a-lifetime shots. And Reece, poor Reece, sat under the goalposts and did his best to appear ignorant. 'How many runs for a wide again?'

'One!'

'And you get another ball for that, right?'

'Yes!'

'Okay!'

I t's easy to become a know-it-all when travelling, to solve the world's ills from the luxury of a minivan. Why don't these people go to university? Why don't they put their rubbish in the bin? Why don't they just leave? It was no different with the boys we were about to play. Sure, Darjeeling was poor, but this was a week day and they were mucking about like no-hopers. Instead of studying, and carving themselves a brighter future, they were knocking a ball about. They were uneducated school-skippers who had no idea how important it was to learn, develop and grow. Bothered by this, I asked Reece to translate my concerns to a kid who had about as much future as the beggars we had

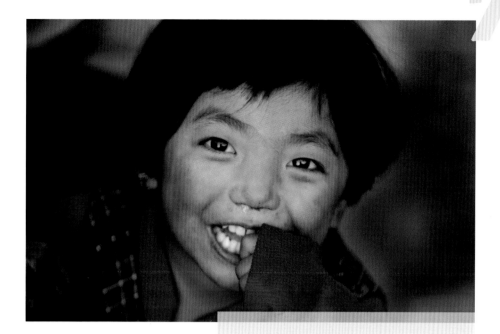

stepped over in Kolkata. Reece did so, but let the good-for-nothing delinquent answer for himself.

'It's the holidays,' said the boy, with the happiest smile I've ever seen.

A smiling face from the streets of Darjeeling. This is one of Brendon's favourite images, mostly because he was missing his daughter who was around the same age.

The kids loved Reece. With his fluent Hindi, he was the star attraction. They continued to crowd and harass, but with the best of intentions. Like anyone passionate about cricket — and in twenty years of following the game I've never seen anything like it — they couldn't bear knowing that Blanket Boy might dock them of a run or, worse, let their mate bat higher up the order.

This was the first game on tour where the boys we were playing really weren't interested in playing a horde of butter-loving gatecrashers. Or at least that's what we thought. Their fake apathy was matched only by their resolve to utterly annihilate us. This became apparent when their opening bowler, Amit, huffed and spluttered his way to the crease, taking out Stew's middle peg with the first ball. It was a nut that would have got anyone out. Then again, as Stew would argue, international cricketers don't have to bat on a pitch more suited to the Calgary Stampede rodeo.

Amit got another wicket with his second ball, and suddenly we were in real trouble. Chasing a solid total of thirty, I stepped up to the plate. It's slightly ridiculous to think that in a friendly backyard game one has such a steely-eyed determination to succeed. But that's blokes: we always have to win. Second is first loser.

John played a short cameo, then I managed to fluke a few boundaries but

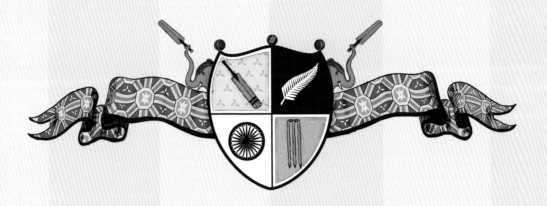

GORKHA STADIUM, DARJEELING

INDIA

Baskar caught Anurag 8
Parag caught (don't know who by) . 10
Amit not out 8
Nikit not out 2
Extras 2

TOTAL 30

BOWLING

Anurag 1-2, Kapis Sharma 0-8, John 1-4,
Stew 0-11, Justin 0-10

BLACK CRAPS

Kapis don't know how out, Reece didn't
write it down 8
John caught (crossed out. Maybe
he was caught. Maybe he wasn't) .. 6
Stew caught (crossed out) 'Sticks
went flying' (That's 'bowled',
Reece) 0
Justin not out 19
Extras 0

TOTAL 33

NEW ZEALAND WINS.
BLACK CRAPS LEAD THE SERIES 3–1.

only because they bowled meaty half-trackers down the leg side. The teenagers, playing hard to get, continued to mumble and mutter and bully the younger boys, a behaviour repeated at many of our matches. A pecking order was established. Some younger ones would try it on with their more mature counterparts, but more often than not would get a hiss, a curse or a whack around the ear. As we handed the Man of the Match hat to one of the friendlier six-year-olds, the older boys sat back with surly faces.

T he younger kids escorted us back to our van and continued to laugh at Stew's shaved head. The back of the stadium smelt of urine, but that didn't stop me needing to contribute to its aroma. Even though we had witnessed thousands peeing wherever they could, I couldn't bring myself to piss in front of a bunch of locals busy playing karom (a tabletop game whose mechanics lie somewhere between billiards and table shuffleboard). Our driver suggested that I ask one of the locals living under the stadium, which appeared to double as a dorm, if I could use their facilities. I was led through a dank, lightless room by a man who appeared to own nothing more than a few blankets and possibly the coldest accommodation on earth. It was a sunny day, yet his room was like a beer fridge. How he survived at night, atop the Himalayas, was anyone's guess. I used his loo.

My bowels, not my nose, were thankful.

Outside, the kids had moved on from Stew's bald head and had spied our — by Western standards — extremely modest minivan. But to them it was as if they had found KITT, the crime-fighting car from *Knight Rider*. They rubbed their hands along its exterior. They peered through its windows. They checked themselves out in its wing mirrors. Then suddenly, as if they all had the same idea at once, they asked if we could take them for a ride.

'Definitely not,' said our driver.

'Definitely!' said the rest of us.

The boys couldn't believe their luck. Their joy was infectious. It got even better once the van started moving. Bursting into a number of Bollywood songs, they yelled to people they knew out the window. Reece translated: 'Isn't this fucking great?' 'Much happiness is coming!'

They still had to get back down the hill once we reached the top, but kids don't care. Kids don't get wet in the rain. They don't get cold. And they certainly didn't mind walking down a tiny hill if it meant they got a free ride. We were all incredibly humbled.

Stacked like cards 2100 metres above sea level, the houses of Darjeeling have a view to die for, but not much else: hot water and electricity are scarce.

Driving past the town's main bazaar ('Carpets?' 'No thanks.' 'Later?' 'Nope.'), we found a bunch of school-age kids playing hacky sack and India's second-most popular sport, soccer. A cricket match, however, was taking main stage in between the markets and the stalls. We watched for half an hour, particularly one left-handed batter named Arougya Dhami. Here was a boy of five with the grace of David Gower and shot selection of Yuvraj Singh. After each masterstroke, he stood back and let the other kids have a go. Then he was straight back into it. His mother, realising that her son was getting some attention, came over, tucked his shirt in, did his jacket up and brushed his hair. 'My husband was a very good player, but my son is better,' she said proudly. 'He will one day play for India.'

John gave him one of our bats. I'm sure he now sleeps with it.

Other kids wanted their photo taken. Snotty-nosed toddlers came up and hugged our legs. Dogs lay in the afternoon heat, glad, finally, to get some warmth out of the Himalayan sun. Mothers, babies on backs, squatted, washing clothes in a dirty bucket. We noticed an absence of young girls.

We kept bowling. Then I had a bat and hit the ball into a nearby hole. 'No, no,' said a boy, following me as I attempted some backyard cricketing etiquette. 'Don't go in there,' he said. 'Very bad. Golden water.'

I looked down the hole, it obviously being where one 'makes toilet'. He was right. Vicky could stay there.

Darjeeling's streets are either narrow, steep or narrow and steep. It's not uncommon to have to manoeuvre a five-point turn to squeeze past an illegally double-parked vehicle, or a donkey with an attitude problem. So by the time we arrived at the foot of another abrupt, heavily crowded lane — which led to a Muslim school, where there was another game in progress — our driver was beginning to realise he was wasting his time trying to make us visit a carpet shop. (Some of these guys were slow learners.)

The game in question was run by an Indian Harry Potter lookalike. He was a short student with a quick wit and an acerbic tongue. A sparkling new Vicky made an appearance, and within seconds was split in half. Stew hit the next one off a nearby cliff: an instant dismissal.

When the ball rolled off, a mother laden with child ran after it. 'Come on, shaky shaky, bum bum!' said Harry Potter.

He noticed us laugh. We tried not to, but hearing him was akin to hearing your two-year-old saying 'fuck' every time she tried to say 'truck'. Unfortunately our suppressed sniggers gave him licence to continue. Honestly, watching this poor woman — with a baby on her back (and clearly bigger worries) — negotiate her way down a slippery bank just to retrieve our stupid ball was totally surreal. Harry Potter kept up his limited, yet blue, English vocabulary. And we five grown men who knew we shouldn't be laughing couldn't stop.

'Come on, fucky fucky up the arse!' he hollered at her. The other boys were now cackling with delight. We tried to look away. It felt like trying not to laugh in class, or around the dinner table with your siblings.

When Thick-Skinned Woman (who had, amazingly, located our ball among the debris and rubbish at the base of the cliff) finally threw it back, Harry Potter yelled, 'Thank you, Mr Cunt!'

As Harry Potter continued to try to teach us Hindi swear words, we witnessed a new Wasim Akram in the making. This kid was quick, whippy, fearless. You couldn't get the ball off him. He seemed content to bowl all afternoon. Maybe he thought we were talent scouts. In between balls, I asked him what year he was in.

'I've just finished my BSc,' he smiled, girlishly pushing his shoulder-length hair behind his ears. 'I have a new job in the state of Sikkim.'

'How old are you?'

'Twenty-three.'

As usual the kids looked a lot younger than they were. But they grew up too fast.

Meanwhile, Harry Potter's bossiness, and the fact that every time we hit the ball it rolled into more 'golden water',

meant we had long since given up trying to make this a legitimate match. Reece didn't have to score. I have never seen him look so happy.

'Oh, Christ,' said Stew, looking at his watch. 'We've got to be back at the Windermere.'

'Why?' we asked.

'High tea,' he said, heading for the van.

'Are you kidding?' said Brendon, taking photos of kids taking slip catches. 'I'd like to stay a bit longer. I'm getting some great shots.'

'Come on!' Stew persisted. 'It said high tea is served at three.'

'We're going to leave the very reason we came here for a cup of tea?'

'Yep.'

'Seventeen hours on a plane, ten hours to get up that stinking hill, seven thousand feet above sea level, and we're going to leave it all just so we can have a cucumber sandwich?'

'There's scones,' said Stew.

'I'm in,' said Reece. 'Let's go.'

Back at the Windermere, we followed the morning suits and spotless white gloves through to Daisie's sitting room. There we sat, like great bloody ponces, with our legs crossed and lips pursed. This really was going from the sublime to the ridiculous. One minute we were fetching a manky ball from an Indian sewer, the next we were in a scene from *Upstairs, Downstairs*.

Previous page: The world-famous Darjeeling Himalayan Railway — nicknamed the Toy Train — is one of only two such trains still working in the world. An engineering marvel in the world of miniature railways, it covers more than eighty kilometres in about eight hours. Trainspotter heaven for John and Brendon!

TOY TRAINS IN THE HIMALAYAS

Advertisement in local paper: 'HIV (+) man looking for HIV (+) bride. Jain (28 years), 6 foot, good looking, Gujarati. B.E. Well settled, caste no bar. No dowry.'

'Jain? Would that be his name?' I asked Reece at breakfast.

'No, Jain is a religion,' he replied, before asking for more butter for our toast. 'Jains do not believe in harming any living creature. In fact, many wear a muslin face mask so they do not breathe in any insects. And they sweep the ground in front of them so they don't stand on anything they might kill. Jains run India's banking and finance sector as they believe this is the only industry that does not harm animals. The most extreme Jains, the Digamber sect, will not eat any root vegetables — onions, carrots, garlic etcetera — as they believe eating the roots will kill the plant.'

'So what's a Gujarati?' I asked, working my way through the ad.

'A person from the western state of Gujarat,' said Reece. 'They are typically renowned businessmen and usually militant vegetarians, from the home state of Mahatma Gandhi. Gujaratis are the most internationally settled Indians, found in every corner of the globe. In fact, any Indian who runs a dairy in New Zealand is probably from Gujarat.'

'And caste is like a pecking order, isn't it?'

'Every Hindu is separated into one of hundreds of castes which defines their position in society — originally developed by Aryans two thousand-odd years back to keep them on top of the pile. Caste defines occupation, and until the last twenty years virtually no Indian would even entertain the thought they may get a job outside family occupations that have been going on for generations. "Caste no bar" means the groom is willing to consider a bride from any caste group, not necessarily only the one that his family belongs to. Advertising caste in marriage or having a person's caste determine if they are suitable for a job has been illegal since the 1980s but still affects every decision made by most people.'

'And what's "no dowry"?'

'Dowry is officially illegal too, but thought to be a part of at least ninety per cent of all Indian marriages. Traditionally, it was the wealth a bride brought into her new family. After marriage an Indian bride normally has almost nothing more to do with her birth parents — she becomes the daughter of her husband's parents. In fact, my Hindi teacher, supposedly from a progressive family, had never stayed a night at her own parents' place since she was married forty years ago as that would make it look as though her in-laws were not looking after her. Dowry is usually demanded by the husband's parents and, although it's supposed to belong to the bride, after marriage she usually loses the lot. Poor families these days usually make dowry demands such as motor scooters, colour TVs and always lots of gold. The minimum is usually one lakh, which is one hundred thousand rupees. Wealthy families will probably end up with a holiday home in Goa!'

Isn't that engine at the wrong end of the train?

'So in this case,' I said, pointing to the page, 'the poor bloke with HIV says "no dowry". I'm guessing he doesn't want any of the girl's junk from her last place?'

'In reality, it probably means he's so sick he's happy just to have her.'

As we ate, an elderly man from Missouri walked around the Windermere dining room waving a letter of complaint. How sweet, we thought; and what a complete waste of energy in India.

We were long overdue for a Delhi Belly round-up. 'How's everyone feeling this morning?' I asked.

'Solid as a rock,' said Stew.

'Fine,' said John.

'Mmghmmhg,' said Reece, with a mouthful.

'Bit gassy,' said Brendon.

This I knew, as Brendon lived in close proximity to Reece and me (although not as close as our original porter intended). As much as we took the piss out of his ailing stomach, we did actually need him. We knew from watching Brendon try to get the ultimate picture while running around with lenses the size of an

elephant's hard-on that he had stamina, endurance, and an obvious love for his craft. He was pretty good at his job.

Not that we'd tell him; that's for girls.

After breakfast it was time to leave, which was sad, as we'd become strangely attached to the Windermere. There was one final laugh before we left our room, in the form of a typed note left on our beds: 'If you need a sock darned, a button sewn on, or a stitch put in a seam, please send the article for repair to Kan-chi through your room maid. Kan-chi sews for love. Her service is free.'

While having a few throw-downs in the Windermere's car park, we heard a loud bang, identical to a gunshot. The security guard, seeing the slightly worried looks on our faces, said, 'It's fireworks.' Yeah right, we thought, fireworks in a place with a strong military presence and recent assassinations.

Apart from getting down the mountain and catching an overnight train to Varanasi, this morning was all about Darjeeling's infamous train. Three members

of the group showed no excitement; two could barely contain it. The Darjeeling Himalayan Railway, nicknamed the 'Toy Train', is a two-foot narrow-gauge railway that runs from Siliguri to Darjeeling. Operated by the Indian Railways, it was built between 1879 and 1881 and is about eighty-six kilometres long. What gets most folk excited is the fact that the train is still powered by a steam engine. Since 1999, the railway has been a World Heritage Site as listed by UNESCO.

Our train spotters couldn't stop clicking, and the good news was that when the train puffed, John could too. Both snappers were in seventh heaven, unlike the rest of us. OK, it was an old train and it still had steam. Whoop-dee-doo. It hardly spun my wheels or, it seemed, Stew's or Reece's.

As we left Darjeeling, we drove past school kids, spick and span in their pristine uniforms; between open-air stalls selling pots and pans, tape decks and packets of potato chips past their use-by date; and through precipitous alleyways traversed by stoic young and old for centuries. Tourist jeeps lined up, as if in a car yard, waiting for adventurous punters to arrive. And, once again, we hoofed it past a poor bugger on his bike, minding his own business, who got a horn in the ear

Above: A typical Indian street-cricket ball, consisting of plastic bags and gravel bound together with a bicycle tyre. Learn to hit one of these and you can do anything.

Left: The MCG (Miniature Cricket Ground), Darjeeling. A better backyard cricket arena you couldn't hope for. Sadly, the playing surface resembled a beach, and as a result we couldn't chase down a score of four!

because he deserved it.

Before we made further strides, however, we wanted one final game in the Queen of the Hills. And it didn't take long to find one. Little did the Black Craps know, we were about to make history — for all the wrong reasons.

Just above road level, eight youngsters were playing in the ultimate backyard cricket arena: a fenced-off piece of dirt about the size of a tennis court with a view stretching all the way to the clouds. It was the sort of ground every backyard cricketer dreams of: an MCG (Miniature Cricket Ground) with high mesh fences to stop sixes, and a special little roadside entrance where you could march in when it was your turn to bat.

We wondered why such a seemingly prime piece of real estate wasn't being used for something more. Then we saw the reason: a power substation the size of Homer Simpson's office hummed greedily by the long-on boundary. It was protected by a flimsy barbed wire fence, but had live wires all over the show. This patch of land was probably fine to risk one's young life playing sport on, but not to inhabit. Indeed, thoughts of the boy from the paper who lost both arms and legs retrieving a cricket ball made us a little anxious.

But not for long. 'Have a bowl, shall we?' said Stew, opening the van door.

We entered the pocket-sized stadium to be greeted by a fine young boy named Pramay. 'What is your name please?' he asked.

'Justin,' I replied, as a dirty hand was placed in mine.

'You are welcome here, Justin. Are you happy?'

Pramay took us on a short tour of his playing square, like a real estate agent showing off an open home. He could barely wait to start the match, and we were heartened to discover, for the first time on the trip, a local who wanted to be on our side. The ball, however, was to be our main obstacle. Filled with rocks, and wound with a variety of rubber bands, it wasn't the easiest thing to smash for six — not least because of the spa pool-sized crater in front of the popping crease. (This pitch was clearly used every day of the year.)

A perfect amphitheatre, with mums and dads watching from the roadside . . . this match had all the makings of being a cracker. Sadly, it was to produce the lowest score in the history of cricket. Stew and I could only watch — by a buzzing, prehistoric transformer — as our batsmen, set a grand total of four after some decidedly average batting by India, failed to hit the rock/string/rubber/globe thing they called a ball. As we ran out of overs, our players ran out of options.

Sunbam, the captain, bowled beautifully, taking wickets with ease, mums and dads clapping from the sideline. Despite this being by far the easiest game Reece had to record to date, he failed to write down who scored what. He had, however, taken to writing down India's ages, which would be useful for Wisden but not for the Black Craps. These were bright and wonderfully happy kids. And they loved their cricket.

After the match I interviewed Pramay, as if we were on TV. 'Favourite player?'

'Stephen Fleming.'

'Favourite subject?'

'History.'

'What do you want to be when you're older?'

'A doctor, so I can help people.'

'Do you have a family?'

'Yes, my dad drives a truck — and my mum is at home.'

As was invariably the case on this trip, most of the kids wanted to keep playing. But we had places to see and games to lose. Stew and I didn't get a bat, but did have the pride of knowing that we had set a world record: the lowest-ever total in the backyard form of the game. The kids couldn't stop waving as we left.

DARJEELING, WEST BENGAL

INDIA

Monish (12) no scores, no squiggles,
   no nothing
Sunbam (10) . . . .
Chiring (12) . . . .
Brijesh (11) . . . .
Monish (11) . . . .
Pryash (11) . . . .
Extras 0

TOTAL. 4

BLACK CRAPS

Abishek (10) . . . .
Pramay (12) . . . .
Chogel (11) . . . .
Extras 0

TOTAL. 3

BOWLING

1-1 (that's all that Reece wrote down)

INDIA WINS.
BLACK CRAPS LEAD THE SERIES 3–2.

henever I go for a beer with my father these days, I notice that he swears a lot more than usual, as if the words have been wrestling and building up inside his mouth all these years and need to make a m*therf*cking getaway. His logic is sound: Mum doesn't need to hear it; his son can cope. Those in the Goldfish Bowl couldn't help but notice the same phenomenon happening to Stew. Every second word was 'fuck'.

'Geez, we've gone through some fucking butter.'

'Did you fucking see the fucking steam coming out of that fucking train?'

'Fuck me, do they have to fucking piss everywhere?'

'Are you still reading that fucking book, Justin?'

We could have started a swear jar, but where's the fun in that? The Goldfish Bowl was, after all, a no-holds-barred, no-topic-out-of-bounds, piss-taking portable juggernaut of filth and non-decorum.

That's right — it was home.

As the altitude dropped, the temperature rose and the outlook changed from inhospitable living to one where you could make one off the land. I wondered why it was that return trips always seemed quicker. Maybe because you knew what you were in for. Crawling down the mountain was no different. And it forced us to relax. Even John, who I'm sure can't sit still on the toilet, learned the chords C, F and G on my daughter's ukulele. Stew was just happy if there were horns, Brendon sucked in and recorded the scenery, and Reece did his best to become his digestive system's number-one arch rival.

'What the hell are those?' Stew asked as Blanket Boy opened a steaming bag of street food from a nearby stop.

'Momos!' he said. 'Beef dumplings,' he continued, when faced by blank looks. He stuck one in his mouth. 'Momos . . . with an inedible chilli sauce. Yikes!'

'Why the hell are you eating them?' I asked.

'They're beautiful!' he said, passing the bag. 'Do you want some?'

'You'll pay for it tomorrow.'

'Where's your sense of adventure?' asked Reece, finishing the bag in record time. Each momo, near boiling point, ping-ponged around inside his gob. 'You're right though,' he muttered, rummaging around the van floor for something to wash it down with. 'I'll probably pay for it tomorrow.'

A match that never got going due to Darjeeling's propensity for lost balls. (Mountainsides will do that.)

Half an hour later we stopped to join a TV shop worker watching the current India-Pakistan series. Stretched out on his shop mattress — with his six-month-old son in his arms — the most relaxed-looking man in the universe must have wondered why the gods had chosen him to have a job where he could mix business with pleasure. In between overs, we asked for some local Hindi tunes for the Goldfish Bowl.

'Sugam Pokhrel?' Reece asked, looking at the CD cover. 'Nepalese artist?'

'Yes,' said the owner, eyes not leaving the TV.

'Pirate?' Reece asked.

'Course he's not a pirate, you fuckwit,' I said. 'He's a singer.'

Reece knew I was being an idiot. He was, of course, alluding to the fact that so much music in Asia — and around the world for that matter — is illegally copied and sold. He repeated the question. 'Pirate?' he asked the man with the easiest job in the world.

'One hundred and fifty rupees,' repeated the man.

'Pirate?'

'One hundred and fifty.'

'Pirate?'
'One hundred and fifty.'
And so on.
'He's actually a singer,' I reiterated, as we walked back to the van.
'Shut up,' said Reece.

One thing was becoming certain on this odyssey: the more we saw the other balls being used for cricket, the more we came to appreciate dirty old Vicky. A case in point were the three young occupants of a shack we discovered on a main road, using little more than a rock wrapped in a plastic bag. Their pitch was the driveway, their wicketkeeper a main highway. Granted, cars could do little more than fifty kilometres an hour on such a snake-like thoroughfare, but this was one of those situations — which occur a lot in India — where you want to suggest the toddlers get off the road and go inside to read a book. Back to your safe little lives, Cotton-Wool Westerners. This was the sort of place you could shoot a movie, but not one where you could live. Remoteness and loneliness went hand in hand.

I had begun to enjoy interviewing each game's Man of the Match. Today's, held after a quick few hits into oncoming traffic, was with Vivek Pradhan, an eleven-year-old whose favourite players were India's Mahendra Singh Dhoni, Sri Lanka's Malinga the Slinger and, rather bizarrely, England's Alastair Cook. His mates yelled, 'Britney Spears!' when I asked after his favourite artist. But he stuck to his guns, naming Himesh, an Indian pop star, instead. And although his preferred career choice was to be like Kris, a superhero gaming character, he'll probably have to put up with career plan number two: the Indian Army.

The Goldfish Bowl continued on its way, past more safety signs clearly written by government workers with too much time: 'If married, divorce speed' and 'Hurry burry spoils the curry'. Soon we were in New Jalpaiguri and ready to jump on an Indian overnight train. We sat in the first-class lounge — which consisted of one small table, a broken fan and a toilet which smelled as though you were inside someone's arse — and everyone seemed in equally agreeable moods. This was to be our sanctuary while we waited for the delayed North-east Express to Varanasi. It was a hovel, but at least our bags were safe. Stew wrote in his diary, John paid the equivalent of a month's Indian wages to get his shoes shined, and I attempted another chapter of *Shantaram*. I had become obsessed with the author's description of a bar in Mumbai named Leopold's, an open-air pub where expats smoked cigars, drank cocktails and

committed dodgy deeds. It was the focal point of the novel and he described it brilliantly, but after 546 pages out of 817, reading was beginning to feel like homework. The others had started giving me

Opposite page: Darjeeling locals shoot the breeze beside a homemade fire. Behind is a typical Himalayan roadside stall.

Left: One of the many roadside signs. Others made about as much sense, but at least provided laughs on a long drive.

grief for travelling with a book resembling a brick. I saw it differently: at least I had a weapon handy should Reece choose to snore again.

This, however, wasn't to be an issue once we eventually boarded the North-east Express, an hour and a half late. With only four to a compartment (and there being five of us) we kindly let Reece loose among his own people. The same people who, despite Reece's insistence, still didn't wear blankets, and still definitely didn't eat soup with their fingers. When food did arrive, shortly after we departed, we watched him slop and slurp his way through runny dhal and vegetable curry. We glanced around the carriage: not one Indian was using his fingers.

'It's the twenty-first century, Reece,' said Stew, passing him a plastic knife and fork.

'It's called respect, Stew,' fired back Reece.

'Anyone want my chicken?' asked Brendon, looking queasy.

eing on a train is a bit like camping — you have a lot of evening to fill before it's lights out. Luckily, once Reece completed licking his lumpy yoghurt-drenched fingers he had stories about our destination. 'Back in 1993, when I lived in Varanasi,' he said, 'I was having a wash in the Ganges . . .'

'You washed in the Ganges?' John asked, looking up from his book.

'Yeah. Every day.'

'But isn't it full of dead people?' I asked.

'And dogs,' said Reece. 'And babies. Anyway, I was scrubbing away, and as I stood up, my foot went straight through someone's body.'

'A live body?'

'A dead body! The upper torso floated to the surface and went downstream.'

'Was it just a skeleton?' I asked.

'No, it was still fleshy.'

Reece loved the look on our faces. And now he was on a roll. 'It's not as bad as the day a dog swam out and grabbed a dead baby and brought it back onto shore, and all the other dogs came and ripped it to pieces.'

A collective, 'No.'

'Yes,' said Reece. 'It was one of the worst things I've ever seen. The baby was dismembered and the dogs were all fighting over it. All I remember is the length of the poor thing's intestines.'

'Did people watch it?'

'No,' said Reece, 'this is India. They just went about their daily business.'

We sat in silence as the train rumbled alongside a setting sun.

'You're not making me want to visit this river,' Brendon said.

'Me neither!' said Stew.

To non-cricket lovers this might look like three strangely placed twigs. To Indians it suggests hope, fun and a battle of titanic proportions.

'I want to go back to the Windermere,' I added.

'Oh, don't be so silly,' said Reece, staring out the train window, a wistful look in his eye. 'Varanasi's great.'

Every now and again, a mobile phone beeped. A text from home. An embarrassed smile from the recipient. Not once, even from the peaks of the Himalayas, did we fail to get crystal-clear reception. It put the networks at home to shame, especially as some mobile phone companies were offering deals for one rupee (about four US cents) a minute. Having such accessible means of communication in such a foreign environment was a great comfort. Which was just as well really, as we were about to receive urgent news from home that would change the trip completely.

SIX

Previous page: As his family has done for seven hundred years, Baap
(Reece's adopted Indian father) rows one of his twelve boats along the
sacred River Ganges.

AMONG THE DEAD IN THE CITY OF LIFE

The night passed and no gear was stolen. Brendon was particularly anxious about his camera equipment, but our see-through, ripped curtain was clearly an extreme line of defence. Everyone claimed they slept well. One small mercy had been the lack of snoring, despite John sharing Reece's affliction. (It must be a second-cousin thing.) Stew, however, who always roomed with John, was savvy when it came to counteracting the issue, having invested in state-of-the-art earplugs which blocked even the most fervent sleep thief. On more than one occasion, as Reece threatened to lift our ceiling at 3 am, I seriously considered borrowing them. But that would probably have been pushing the bounds of friendship a little too far.

Outside the window, a grey fog sat on dew-covered fields. Unimpressed buffalo glanced at the train with contempt. Tiny fires glowed, surely not warming anyone, and, as always, people sat among the reeds performing their morning ablutions.

'Reece, what are the rules about pissing and shitting in this place?' we asked.

'There are no rules,' said Reece.

'So you can go wherever you want?'

'Pretty much.'

'Do people go in the same place every day?'

'Probably.'

I glanced at my watch: 7.41 am.

'What about women? Do they squat in front of men?'

'No, they probably get up at 4.30.'

It was another example of how tough life must be for women in India. Take marriage: while it has always been immensely important, the institution has traditionally treated women as less than equals. Often dowries overwhelm poor families struggling to make payments. In India's largest cities, newspapers are full of stories of 'dowry deaths', in which new brides are murdered or driven to commit suicide as a result of bullying for a dowry payment by the groom or his family. And although dowries were made illegal in 1961, they, and dowry deaths, are still commonplace.

The prospect of a shower and a feed kept our spirits high as we dressed in our tiny compartment. Soon we were off the North-east Express and inhaling coal, a smell I would never have associated with India.

'The changes have been phenomenal, and slightly scary, since I was here twenty years ago,' said Reece, watching a cow try to chew a plastic bag. 'Those guys, for example,' he said, pointing at the bony heifer. 'They used to be the perfect natural vacuum cleaner, mopping up everything from food scraps to cigarette packets. But that all changed in '94 with the advent of the plastic bag. The poor buggers can't digest them. Add to that the fact that India's population has doubled and you have problems.'

'Doubled?' Brendon asked. 'Since when?'

'Three hundred million people in the last seventeen years. An extra twenty-two million people a year. That's an Australia every year.'

Wasim was our new guide. He possessed a ready smile and a trendy pink shirt with brown pants, a little tight around the bum. We headed towards our new Goldfish Bowl, another white van with 'TOURIST' plastered over the front, through the early morning bedlam of Varanasi's railway station. News had filtered through of a bomb that had torn through a New Delhi-bound high-speed train travelling in north-east Assam state, killing five passengers. A little-known militant tribal group, the Adivasi National Liberation Army, had claimed responsibility. Adivasis, the descendants of indentured labourers brought in to work on the tea plantations in the nineteenth century, had been displaced and wanted the government to include them on the list of what are called 'Scheduled Tribes', making them eligible for reserved jobs and places in education. As we tried to watch more of the report on a shop owner's fourteen-inch TV set, people in the railway station continued to yell, curse, laugh, beg, sweat, heave, push, pull, tug, wait, hawk, eat, snatch, hug, peer, spit, jostle and pray.

Hindus believe that the membrane seperating heaven and earth is at its closest to earth at Varanasi.

In other words, it was just another Tuesday morning in India.

ere is where I attempt to explain why Varanasi, or Benares as it was formerly known, is considered the godliest, holiest, most spiritual place on earth. For a start, it's the only point where, after leaving the Himalayas, the Ganges turns and flows directly south to north, which it does for about ten kilometres. This is believed to be the Mother Ganges turning towards her Himalayan home. Hindus believe that each range in the Himalayas represents a flowing dreadlock of Shiva's hair. Shiva is pretty important, if his title Lord of Destruction is anything to go by. Legend has it that Shiva married his first wife, Meenakshi, after she lost her earring and he helped her find it. (A likely story.) When she died, he cremated her in Varanasi, but because she had married a guy with a fair dose of religious clout, she would go directly to Nirvana. (For those of you who — like me —associate Nirvana

Dawn of a new day on the steps of the Ganges.

only with Kurt Cobain, the actual meaning is moksha or liberation.) By cremating his wife in Varanasi and guaranteeing her liberation, Shiva also guaranteed that any Hindu cremated on the Ganges would never have to go through the cycle of rebirth again. (Which can be a right bloody hassle, let's be honest.) Varanasi has been a literal tirtha, or crossing place, of the Ganges for at least five thousand years. Metaphorically, tirtha also refers to a crossing point between heaven and earth. Hindus believe that the membrane separating heaven and earth is at its closest to earth anywhere on the planet at Varanasi.

Our first experience of Varanasi, however, was of watching a man pissing into a roadside pile of rubbish. We were caught in a traffic jam shaped like an egg timer. For some reason, the busiest stretch of road was also the thinnest, choked by a swathe of Tata trucks carrying coal trying to squeeze through gaps half their width.

And yes, you guessed it, the horns were back. 'Thought something was missing,' laughed Stew.

'Back in Toot-land,' I said.

Meanwhile, the Urinator was still attempting to finish his business. It was turning out to be the longest piss in the world. He kept nervously looking behind to see if his bus was still there. The driver beeped. The Urinator kept pissing, shaking his member in a futile attempt to hurry things along. But he was still pissing. The driver beeped again, slowly edging forward. Now, when the Urinator turned to look at the full bus, he didn't move just his neck but his whole body, urging his whole being to excrete what liquid leftovers remained. Rush hour commuters, ourselves included, couldn't help but look at his member. It was like witnessing the aftermath of a car crash: you knew you shouldn't look, but had to. The Urinator didn't care. He had a job to do. The traffic was now moving. His driver had no choice but to join them. Shake, shake, shake went the Urinator. He wouldn't have time to finish so tugged a few final times on his run to the bus, poking his member away only once he reached the steps.

'No rules,' I said to Reece.

'No rules,' he confirmed.

We drove past a main-street abattoir where buffalo were being forced into a prehistoric-looking killing chamber. There was so much blood and frenzied activity that I wanted to go in for a look, but that would really have tipped Wasim over the edge. Our carpet-shop-loving guides struggled enough as it was with our bizarre leisure activities; they hardly needed an ignorant city boy asking if he

could watch a bull being slaughtered.

'Look at the poor fucker,' said Stew the farmer, watching a cow do everything she could to avoid an inevitable end. 'They fucking hate the smell of fucking blood.' (His swearing was still at fever pitch.) The Goldfish Bowl continued its way past rubbish dumps and into the welcoming arms of the holiest city on earth.

'Still a shit-hole,' said John, clearly having not changed his views on Varanasi since his last visit.

'Oh, come on, John,' said Reece. 'It's like coming home!'

'To you, maybe,' replied John. 'To me, it's a shit-hole.'

I t is one of life's wonders how breakfast and a hot shower can erase any unease caused by a fourteen-hour train ride. As we waited for the Goldfish Bowl in the hotel forecourt, we felt relaxed and happy. That is, until Reece approached Brendon with the look of a school teacher about to give one of his students a serve.

'I've been meaning to say this for a while,' said Reece, pointing to Brendon's bare knees. 'You shouldn't be wearing half-pants.'

'What do you mean, half-pants?' Brendon asked.

'Shorts,' said Reece.

'Why the hell not?'

'It's disrespectful.'

'Disrespectful, my arse!' I said.

'Do you see any Indians wearing half-pants?' Reece asked.

Brendon and I looked around. Long slacks everywhere.

'It's like wearing your underpants in public,' said Reece.

'You're joking.'

'I'm not. Look at John, he's been to India. He knows you don't wear half-pants. Isn't that right, John?' Reece asked, looking around for his second cousin.

'Jesus Christ!' we heard John muttering in the distance. 'Worst pollution in the world and you can't suck on a cigarette when you're checking into your hotel. Rack and ruin, I tell you.'

For the rest of the trip, Brendon and I decided that we would wear half-pants whenever possible. Not out of disrespect for the Indians; more out of spite for Blanket Boy.

> Indian cows are used to the rhythm of the city. They are believed to be a symbol of the earth as they give so much yet ask for nothing in return.

Brendon had heard via one of his mates that there was a cemetery in Varanasi where the locals often played cricket. This was a sitting duck for five blokes who favoured finding exotic locations to whack a six over drinking tea in silk shops. Finding the cemetery, however, was easier said than done. Our taxi driver managed to find one, but it was frequented by dead people, not backyard cricketers. Not that it stopped us looking for players. Wading through knee-high grass, we voyeuristically hovered over headstones. Three dodgy-looking locals loitered. Several headstones had been pinched, and those remaining were neglected or smashed. A 'caretaker' soon saw the whities with the cameras and cricket bat and saw an opportunity. After a chat in Hindi with Blanket Boy, it was confirmed that the caretaker wanted money from us.

'What for?' John asked.

'He's the caretaker. He thinks we should pay him for the privilege.'

I looked around this overgrown, desolate, depressing final resting place. 'How about he caretake it then?'

It was our lucky day. Reece gleaned the information from our driver that there was another cemetery in town. 'You want to go there?' he asked. 'Or you want to go see carpet?'

'Cemetery please!' we said in unison.

Our driver shook his head and put his van into first. As we crawled through another litter-filled mass of mess and mayhem, I tended to side with John: Varanasi wasn't exactly Vienna, but knowing we would be on the Ganges by nightfall excited every one of us. A few windows were left open in the Goldfish Bowl and a sweet, slightly sickly aroma soon filled the space between us.

'What is that smell?' I asked.

'It's a smell covering another smell,' said John.

'It's life!' said Reece.

'It smells like shit,' said John.

Despite thinking we were homicidal maniacs, our driver came through with the goods, parking outside the nondescript, run-down entrance to the second cemetery of the morning. He then, via Reece, introduced us to Mr Thomas, the cemetery's Roman Catholic priest and caretaker. The irony didn't escape us that we were about to play cricket, in a cemetery, in the City of Life. Indeed, in one of the holiest cities on earth, where most locals choose cremation over burial, it seemed incongruous to be standing in the middle of a cemetery. But then, this cemetery was hardly a going concern. It was once used by the British Army, and soldiers as well as any immediate family had been buried here. What we didn't realise was that Mr Thomas had been trying to stop the cricket-playing so he could make it a more reputable place. Until we arrived.

Before long, the puns came flooding out:

'We'll have some stiff competition today.'

'I bet the game will be dead boring.'

'People will be dying to play.'

Mr Thomas herded us through the cemetery gates, past his modest but tidy hut. A boy grabbed our bat. 'Match?' he yelped. 'Match?'

'Yes,' we said. 'Match.'

Sprinting over to the makeshift pitch, the boy pushed whoever was batting out of the way. We soon joined him and within minutes a multitude of kids surrounded us. They came out of the woodwork like meerkats. Some, especially

The Black Craps' cemetery match attracted eager onlookers, the graves doubling as both wickets and fielders.

the older boys, would make most international sides; their style and flair was enviable. And yet, amid such lunacy, gravestones and tombs. We ambled through the grounds, fascinated, saddened:

> MARSHA Dt of birth — 22.8.96; Dt of death — 23.9.98
> IRENE Dt of birth — 4.1.98; Dt of death — 7.1.98
> With lots of love and kisses, papa and mummy

> MARIA The beloved wife of Edward Robbins who died at Benares on 24th October, 1858, aged 42 years and 7 months. She died as she had lived; a true Christian, a fond and faithful wife, and affectionate mother.

> IN MEMORY OF Caroline Aldus Robbins, infant daughter of the above, who died on 2nd October, 1858, on the passage up the river Ganges, from Calcutta to Benares. Aged 11 months.

The fact that cricket was to be played above someone's dead ancestors didn't seem to bother anybody. After all, tombstones make for perfect stumps. And why not play on top of people's graves? Is it any more disrespectful than burning a body then throwing it into the drink? Indeed, one got the feeling the soldiers buried here would have endorsed their sacred place being used for the sacred game.

As usual, the match took an age to start. But at least the kids were willing to play for the Black Craps. Maybe the thought of actually playing was worth being embarrassed for. Whatever their reasoning, Stew and I were ecstatic: finally we had some depth. As they taught us the local rules ('third row of graves is four runs'), proud mums ordered the younger kids to go away and put on their Sunday best. They returned with combed hair and ironed trousers up to their armpits. Their taller, older, scruffier-dressed counterparts looked as though they were designed for cricket. They breathed the game. As soon as a ball was tossed their way, they took on the personas of Ganguly, Laxman and Rahul Dravid.

We bowled first, and badly. Square cuts soon ricocheted off tombstones. Sixes gave the crows something to worry about. Their opening batsman, Anu Khan — high back-lift and exquisite footwork — walloped us over goats, past buffalo lazing in the midday sun and finally, and to our horror, right into a make-shift rubbish dump in the far corner of the graveyard. The result: they batted like Australia; we bowled like Zimbabwe. Blindfolded.

India scored sixty-seven for four on a goat track. It seemed a formidable total. The outfield was stony, dry and dusty. The pitch wasn't much better. But this was their ground — they knew every quirk. Goats and sheep grazed, unfazed. Kids in school uniforms gathered on stone walls surrounding the cemetery. World Cup-

Ask any sports photographer what they really want and the reply will always be the same: 'jubo' (jubilation). And there was no shortage of it at the Kabristan (cemetery) Sporting Club, Varanasi, when John lost his wicket to Kham for six.

style celebrations ensued whenever a wicket was taken. Every one of these kids wanted to succeed. They wanted it bad. And even though they'd never admit, as often seems to be the case in a selfish game like cricket, they secretly hoped their mate would get out so they too could face the Kiwis.

As always, while all of this nonsense was going on mid-pitch, Reece continued to be smothered, swamped and harassed by locals. Today it wasn't only his shortcomings with the scorebook which were to be tested, but also his patience. A woman who, when not blocking his view of the match, kept asking for money,

claimed that a shot by one of the Kiwis had struck her son in the face. He even had the scratch to prove it. She dragged her son over by the arm, squeezing it so hard as to make him cry. 'You hit my son!' she said. 'Pay doctor's bills!' If nothing else, she deserved brownie points for inventiveness.

Reece's adversaries had now become his allies: 'Get away, woman, he's just trying to score!'

Alas, these off-field antics didn't stop the Black Craps losing, managing a paltry forty-four. All this in spite of the fact that John thumped an aerial straight drive so far that it careered over the long-on boundary and ended up on the surrounding train tracks. Lost ball and a proud jig by John. He then showed his true New Zealand colours by self-destructing on the very next ball. But at least he had his moment in India.

Our 'depth', which initially excited a weakened, some would say desperate,

Black Craps side, consisted of two boys who couldn't hit the ball if it had a bell on it. After John's departure, Stew and I were left to pick up the pieces but, needing more than twenty from the final over, my cemetery-dwelling batting partner, obviously playing for his average, batted as though we were here for a five-day match. Needless to say, our PC 'let's give everyone a bat' theory backfired. India had once more, very cleverly, given us their worst players and we had paid the price. Our opposition, on taking the final wicket, high-fived and celebrated like world champions, taunting and jibing as only winners can.

In this whipping of epic proportions, one player stood out as Man of the Match: Anu Kham, the jandal-wearing master blaster with an unbeaten fifty-two and a selection of shots most international players would give their right arm for. But what really secured the award for him was that when during the third over of the game Vicky split in two, he ran off to get a new one. He returned in record time, probably because he happened to be batting at the time. When presented with his Auckland Aces hat, Anu pulled it on as tightly as a swimming cap, and smiled like a loon. A half-century and a half decent souvenir — not a bad day.

'We beat the Kiwis! We beat the Kiwis!' An exuberant bunch of victors who will sadly remember the Black Craps for all the wrong reasons.

As I faced a few more practice deliveries (or, truth be told, chucks), the ringleader approached and asked if we could please play another game. I agreed to a shortened version as long as they bowled and didn't continue to throw the ball, à la Murali and Harbhajan. (This seemed to be a habit with Indians, particularly in the backyard form of the game where a tennis ball was used.) Just as I was about to inform the others, however, I saw everyone crowd around John. No one was laughing. John was on his phone, which wasn't uncommon. What was odd was that he wasn't cavorting about with a smile on his face, telling stories to the recipient. He lightly kicked the dirt and moved around the cemetery as if to find some privacy. An eerie vibe wafted through the cemetery. A stillness prevailed. Reece shooed away small children keen to get a glimpse of John's mobile.

He had now been speaking for more than ten minutes. Something was wrong. Stew approached me, his eyes a mixture of confusion and sadness. 'Did you hear that?' he asked. 'Anna's dead.'

Anna, John's ex-wife, had been living in Cairo for the past two years. The previous evening she had apparently gone to sleep in her apartment not knowing that a candle was still burning. Sometime during the night her home caught fire

and she died of asphyxiation, her golden retriever, George, by her side. Their daughter, John's only child Nicola, was back in Auckland, completely unaware of what had happened.

This was all too weird. Twenty minutes earlier we had been parading about like idiots. We had laughed and joked and hit tennis balls up trees. Now, walking back to the Goldfish Bowl, we thought about Anna. And death in a cemetery. And our own families. And the trip. And John. And holy shit, can't life just change in a split second? A cemetery, for Christ's sake. In the City of Life.

India's ringleader, unaware of the news, approached me again. 'Game?' he asked once more, throwing the ball from hand to hand.

I couldn't think. 'No, sorry. No game.'

'Please!'

'No, seriously, not now.'

'Short game!'

'We've had some bad news from home.'

He nodded, a look of compassion on his face. 'Oh,' he said, putting his hands together in the prayer position and putting them up to his chin. 'Emergency?'

'Yes,' I said. 'Emergency.'

He placed one hand on his heart. His other non-English-speaking friends were obviously anxious to get another game started. He quickly shut them up, explaining in Hindi what had happened. A look of unease and intrigue showed in their eyes. They shadowed us from the ground, past Mr Thomas' modest hut.

'My family and I are very sorry for your loss,' said Mr Thomas. He opened the sliding door to the Goldfish Bowl and we drove off.

One thing was clear: John would have to somehow get back to New Zealand to be with his daughter. Later we learned that he would have to go to Cairo — during Eid, the busiest time in the Muslim calendar — to collect Anna's body, and then attend her funeral two days before Christmas.

He had never liked Varanasi.

Three goats, one batting. (Yes,
Brendon wrote that.)

CHOWKI CHUNGI, KABRISTAN, VARANASI

INDIA

Anu Kham not out **52**
Sanjay Khan bowled Emtias Khan . . . **0**
Abdeem Ahmed lbw bowled Faruk **0**
Aklahk Ahmed bowled Faruk **4**
Rinku Kumar bowled Stew **0**
Jamil Khan not out **0**
Khalik Ahmed run out **0**
Extras **11**

TOTAL **67**

BOWLING

Rahul Paul 0-15, Faruk Khan 2-10, Emtias
   Khan 1-8, Tiger Pathan 0-10,
   Stew 1-13, Justin 0-11

INDIA WINS MATCH BY 23 RUNS AND LEADS SERIES 3–2.

BLACK CRAPS

Faruk Khan lbw bowled Abdeem
   Ahmed **18**
Emtias Khan caught Anu Kham bowled
   S. Khan (wouldn't get off
   strike!) **9**
Tiger Pathan caught A. Ahmed bowled
   A. Kham (wouldn't get off
   strike!) **4**
John stumped Khalik bowled A. Kham
   (we'll never hear the end of
   that six) **6**
Justin not out **0**
Extras **7**

TOTAL **44**

BOWLING

Anu Kham 0-7, Sanjay Khan 1-13, Abdeem
   Ahmed 1-5, Aklakh Ahmed 1-5, Jamil
   Khan 0-9, Khalik Ahmed 0-5

Varanasi's narrow lanes are
called galis.

SEVEN

Previous page: Wherever there is level ground, there will be cricket,
regardless of the state of the outfield.

LOSING THE PLOT

The taxi ride from the cemetery back to our hotel was one of the most unforgettable of my life, yet I can't remember one thing about it. The poverty and squalid surroundings — usually provoking shock and disbelief — caused no reaction whatsoever. It was as though we were driving on air. Images came and went. Beggars continued to knock on the windows. But we had our own troubles. And yet our shock and sadness for John counted for nothing: it was he who would have to perform tasks over the next week that would test even the most hardened. All we could do was be his mate.

Once back at the hotel, the only thing to do was head for the bar. John would need to be near his phone for the foreseeable future; the least we could do was provide him with whisky. Other than that, we felt like spare pricks at a wedding. I called Amy to ask if she could make some calls on John's behalf. Stew and Brendon called their families too.

The pregnant receptionist started to cry when John, in passing, told her his news. Embarrassed, John recoiled slightly, then attempted to console her. We all felt for him. He was in a tough situation. He and Anna had separated two years before. They had also spent twenty-three years together. On the other hand, however, they were no longer a couple and led separate lives. John was clearly and understandably on another planet as he gulped his whisky. He sat at the bar and checked his emails while the rest of us reflected on a horrifically bizarre day. To try and lift the mood,

Reece proceeded to tell the world's most inappropriate joke. The punchline, possibly the worst part of it, was said with such vigour and volume that it made the couple enjoying a pre-lunch drink to our immediate right get up and leave. Even funnier than the joke was Reece not knowing how inappropriate he was being. Or how loud. It was as if he were a headmaster in front of an assembly. He projected like a thespian. He used language like Billy Connolly. And, perhaps funniest of all, he had absolutely no idea that he'd offended a couple who had spent their entire life savings on a trip to India.

But at least it made us think about other things.

We were always going to visit the River Ganges. Now, given John's situation, it seemed to take on new meaning. He had been on the phone all afternoon and was beat. We convinced him to come. The Goldfish Bowl was waiting outside like a loyal servant. Soon we were back in Mayhem Central driving past a long, gangly man asleep on a busy footpath. All that separated his butt from stone, dust and cigarette papers was a thin layer of sacking, yet he looked as relaxed and unperturbed as a dozing baby, his shoes by his side. How, I wondered, could anyone fall asleep like that? I guess, though, if home was two hours away by rickshaw you couldn't pop off for a lunchtime siesta. You sleep where and when you can. Maybe, without making it sound too frivolous, it's a little like camping: no one ever sleeps well on the first night. After that, you're so tired, you have no choice.

Thoughts like these are never far from your mind in any Indian city. Another recurring issue: how can people live amid such squalor and actually smile? Answer: they have to. If they don't, they die. It's mouse on the treadmill stuff. If you don't get up to shine shoes today, you'll lose your place on the footpath tomorrow. It's the same for the people who weigh people on scales for money. Or clean customers' ears with cotton buds. As Dora says in *Finding Nemo*, 'Just keep swimming.' Amid such poverty, mums were always well dressed and their kids spotless.

Varanasi is said to be the oldest inhabited place on earth. It features so heavily in mythology, fables and childhood stories that it's hard to believe it even exists — until you stand on its riverbanks and find its aura so intoxicating you feel drunk with hope.

Driving through the city had been a storm; this was the calm. We walked down the steps to the Ganges and, for the first time in India, heard absolutely nothing. Not a horn, not a crow, not a truck. From a distance the river looked like a Monet painting; up close, it looked like his long drop. But even with the obvious pollution,

The early morning walk to the Ganges.

this stretch of water came with an undeniable reputation. Maybe the bedlam we had witnessed highlighted the river's tranquillity. Maybe New Zealand was always this quiet and we never appreciated it.

Whatever, Reece was right: this place had spirituality in bucket-loads. It was heaven-like. I haven't visited a more stirring, peaceful place. 'But fuck living here!' I told him. Living there is exactly what he did in 1991. Indeed, part of the reason he wanted to visit the river this afternoon was to book his accommodation for Christmas Eve. (We would leave Mumbai for New Zealand at the conclusion of the trip; Reece had an economy train ticket booked from Mumbai to Varanasi, something you wouldn't wish on your worst enemy.)

'You're going to come back here?' asked a dumbfounded Stew.

'You betcha!' said Reece. 'Christmas in Varanasi, it'll be great.'

'Is that a dead dog in the river?' Brendon asked.

'Probably,' grinned Reece.

'And that bloke's brushing his teeth with the same water?' I asked.

'Uh-huh,' said Reece, nonchalantly. He motioned us to walk down to the river edge where an old Indian couple waited for us.

'This is my Ma and Baap!' said Reece proudly. He and the couple embraced and laughed. I think I even saw Reece cry. He had known Ma and Baap for seventeen years. Keshav, their grown-up son, also hugged Reece and didn't let him go. It had clearly been too long between drinks. Back in 1991 Keshav gave Reece a boat tour of the Ganges. Two years later, when Reece returned there to live, Keshav recognised him instantly, demanding that he accept a free boat ride and meal with his family. At the time, the one-room shack they lived in housed twelve family members and had no electricity or running water. Reece was treated to chapattis and dhal — the staple diet of five hundred million north Indians every night of the week — cooked on a cow-dung fire. As acrid, tear-jerking smoke filled the tiny space, Reece ate delicious food in pitch darkness and, from that moment, became one of the family.

A few months later, Reece bought Keshav a bigger boat so he could start taking bigger groups along the Ganges. And when he got married, Reece bought him ten thousand bricks so the family could add another room to their shack.

'Ten thousand bricks?' I said. 'How much did that cost?'

'About five thousand rupees,' he replied. That's about $US200.

Morning fog shrouds the Ganges, inducing a state of unexpected calm.

Sixteen years later, the family home has expanded somewhat, no doubt to accommodate the twenty-four people who now live there. The single room has expanded to three storeys, with a breezy roof-top terrace, and the cow-dung fire has given way to kerosene burners. There are also windows and, for the five hours a day that Varanasi has power, a couple of light bulbs.

Reece later told me that when Keshav's parents informed him they had found him a bride, Keshav demanded to see her before the wedding (this, of course, being against the rules). Having come from a family who had been boatmen for the past seven hundred years, no less, he was disgusted to find that his bride-to-be came from a flower-growing family. The horror! 'I can't believe it!' he exclaimed. 'I'm going to marry a flower girl.'

Reece the peacemaker tried to calm his adopted brother. 'But, but, a flower girl!' Keshav had insisted. 'Reece, I know which village she comes from. Promise me to take a photo of every flower girl you see, then come back and I might have some idea of who I'm marrying.'

Reece did as he was asked and, thank Shiva, the story ended happily. The boatman married the flower girl, they had two beautiful children and to this day, according to Blanket Boy, are utterly besotted with each other.

We bowed to Ma and Baap, who stood on their boat and welcomed us. We got on board, with our ridiculous cricket bat and even more ridiculous scorebook, Keshav helped his mother off, and we departed. As the sun set, our ears rang with silence. (Thank God the horn sales rep hadn't found the boat owners of the Ganges.) Reece, obviously missing his past vocation, kicked into tour guide-speak upon seeing our first funeral pyre by the water's edge. This was where a body was burned as part of the funeral rites. A good healthy flame was leaping into the sky as family members gathered around a dead loved one.

'When the person dies,' said Reece, 'the family wrap the body, dress it and take it to the temple. Then they bless it and walk it down to the river.' He smiled. 'Then they stand around it and light it.'

Living in Varanasi in 1991 provided Reece with some shocking dinner stories. But look past the funeral pyres and there is something alive and beautiful about the city.

Collective gulps. A body continued to burn fifty metres from our boat. We could hear the crackles and sparks. Everyone else along the river went about their daily business.

'But the best bit,' said Reece, eyes widening, 'is waiting for the skull to explode.'

'What?'

'Piss off!'

'You're pulling our leg!'

'I'm not,' he said. 'The eldest boy, or son-in-law if there is no son, must wait for the body to burn, which can take hours. And he can't leave until the skull explodes. If it doesn't explode, he has to give it a helping hand with a block of wood.'

'A helping hand,' I offered queasily.

'By bashing it in, wallah!'

'And how do you know if the skull has exploded?' I asked.

'Oh, you'd know all right. It's like bloody fireworks when it happens.'

We continued to watch someone else's family member incinerate.

India: it's not a holiday.

ven in the middle of the world's most sacred waterway, no one is safe from touts. Making his way towards our boat was a boy of about ten, expertly rowing to park beside ours. He handed us five floating candles in exchange for fifty rupees. We placed them on the water for Anna. They would float downriver, past cow-laden alleyways, past boys playing cricket on the steps and, weeks later, into Ganga Sagar, a

pilgrim town at the mouth of the Ganges, before finally drifting into the Bay of
Bengal south of Kolkata.

We were all waiting for the skull on shore to explode, but it wasn't going to
happen. We could only imagine what bones and other body parts lay below us in
the waters of the Ganges. Another dead dog floated past, its pock-marked body,
hairless in parts, forcing us to keep our hands firmly above board.

'Not everyone is allowed to be cremated,' said Reece. 'There are five categories
who can't be. Lepers aren't allowed to be because they're still paying the price for
a bad deed in a past life.'

'That's hardly fair. Surely in death they can be spared?'

'Sadly not.'

'Who else can't be cremated?' asked Brendon.

'Pregnant women. Or snake-bite victims, supposedly because that way of death will
send them straight to heaven. Oh, and sadhus can't be cremated either.'

'What are sadhus again?' I asked.

'They're ascetics who leave their families behind and dedicate themselves to the teachings of one of the many saints. Saints occupy what is known as a "mutt", their home base. Every sadhu will be connected to a particular mutt and its resident saint, but will spend most of his time wandering India, visiting all the holy places. They will spend the summer months in the Himalayas cultivating marijuana — in reverence to their lord Shiva, who spent ten thousand years smoking dope in the Himalayas in order to achieve enlightenment.'

'And because of this, they're spared being set alight?' Stew asked.

'Pretty much.'

'Lepers, pregnant women, sadhus and snake-bite victims?' I asked. 'You said there were five categories that can't be cremated.'

'And children under twelve.'

'Why's that?' Stew asked.

'They're innocent. Haven't committed any sins.'

'So if they can't cremate kids,' I asked, not really wanting to know, 'how do they . . . surely they don't just throw them in the river?'

'No, they tie rocks to their feet first.'

Back on dry land, we thanked Baap and Keshav, who reserved a tender embrace for his Kiwi brother. We grabbed our bat and scorebook and watched some boys play cricket on impossible terrain. The steps leading to the Ganges were far from the MCG but these kids found it a more than an adequate place to have a hit. Others played a version of what would otherwise be known as 'Bat Down'. The batter would belt a rock as far as he could and their friend then had to roll it back and hit the cricket bat, which lay at the feet of the hitter.

A pitch consisting of concrete steps didn't deter these kids on the banks of the Ganges, though retrieving the ball from the drink wasn't an enviable task.

At our feet was a skinny mongrel bitch with, no word of a lie, thirty pups suckling from her teats. Clearly she was looking after two other litters as well as her own. As a result, she looked harassed, the pups literally hanging off her, draining what life was left in her dilapidated ribcage of a body. The banquet soon came to an abrupt halt, however, when the bitch finally lost it and took off, pups falling off one by one as she ran. Cue a lumbering, barn-door-sized heifer walking up the passage's cobblestones with an accomplice. Two cows; thirty rat-sized pups. Only one thing could happen, and it did. We moved out of the way. One of the pups wasn't so lucky. One hundred and eighty kilos versus two — hardly a fair fight. The result was a sound which still sticks in my mind. The puppy yelped as if someone had dropped a laptop on its foot. On and on it went, hysterical, careering around in a helpless fit, unable to sit still. It is one of the most affecting things I have ever heard. It's pathetic, I know. A puppy, one of thirty no less, with a mum who hadn't eaten in weeks, was never going to survive, but to be stepped on by a fucking cow! Give me a heart attack any day. Eventually, a dreadlocked European backpacker sprinted over and cradled the screaming pup. She ran back to her accommodation, rocking her newly acquired bad debt as if it were her own.

'Would have been better to wring its neck and throw it in the bloody river,' said the cows' no-nonsense owner. Even the less hardened among us tended to agree.

The Goldfish Bowl got us safely home, where we headed towards food and beer. It had been a big day. A weird day. We felt guilty not being able to do more for John. Death should make your world stop, but in India nothing does. Talk began of how Reece had single-handedly managed to clear the bar with his joke earlier. John, phone (which hadn't stopped ringing all afternoon) by his side, was busy checking emails, making flight plans and receiving words of comfort from friends and family in New Zealand. He found a welcome distraction in a joke which would rival his second cousin's.

'Here's one,' he said, looking at his computer screen. 'Four guys are seen carrying a coffin down Fifth Ave in New York. A guy sees them and thinks, "That's strange." Half an hour later, he sees them again carrying the coffin on the subway. "That's really weird," thinks the guy. An hour later he sees them again in Central Park, to which he finally concludes, "They've lost the fucking plot!"'

The joke provided the release we needed. We looked up to see an affable businessman, immaculately dressed, with his equally stylish wife. Both were in their late fifties or early sixties. He possessed charm and a full head of silver hair, she a girlish figure and shoes worth more than Brendon's camera.

'Where do you suppose I'm from?' he asked us, in what sounded like an Eastern European accent. His wife was smiling.

'Greece?' I asked.

'Nope.'

'Croatia,' said Reece.

'Negative.'

'Russia,' said Brendon.

He nudged his wife, then answered. 'No. I'm from bloody Australia, mate!' He said 'St-ra-ya' the way that only Australians can. It was little wonder he had been so successful in business: he was charismatic, easy to talk to, interested, and made you feel as though you were the only person in the room. He and his wife had been staying with some sultan on some island in some castle the size of Kashmir. Being Australian, and right into cricket, he was incredibly keen on what we were doing.

Whether or not he intended it that way, John had been Dad since Singapore, mainly because he had been looking after the slush fund. The rest of us, apart from Reece, whose Hindi came in useful every now and again, had been the annoying sons. I'll admit that I was particularly skilled on the 'irritating same joke every day/atrocious Indian accent' front. (The sleepwalking didn't help either.) This journey so far had all the makings of a scene from *Lord of the Flies* or an episode of *Survivor*: who would drive who nuts? Whose bowels wouldn't last the journey? More importantly, who would be kicked off the island first? Everyone had believed that it would be me but now, for much sadder reasons, it was John, who was counting rupees and passing them to his much less able second cousin.

'This is mainly for tips,' said John to Reece. 'Be generous to the guys who help you out. Tell the others to fuggoff! There should be enough to last till Mumbai.'

For bigger expenses, Brendon's credit card would be the Black Craps' new currency. Which didn't bother Reece and Stew one bit: 'I'll have another beer if that's the case!' said Stew.

'Piss off,' said Brendon.

'Make mine a vodka,' said Reece. 'Double.'

'Like hell,' said Brendon. With two new Dads, things were going to get messy.

With a belly full of wine and kebabs — effectively the last supper before Brendon's credit card would take a hammering — we sat and reflected on a less than typical travelling day. You could almost see the weight on John's shoulders. We all admired what he was about to do, but wondered how he could. Flying to Cairo to identify Anna, negotiating with Egyptian consulates, completing heinous paperwork and then taking her home to New Zealand was something no one should have to go through. But it was his only option if he wanted the body home with his daughter as soon as possible.

Reece, all out of crass jokes, pushed on with the itinerary. 'Tomorrow we fly to Orchha,' he said. 'You are going to love Orchha. It is, without a doubt, India's best-kept secret. A medieval city built by its Bundela rulers in the sixteenth and seventeenth centuries, and unlike anything you've ever seen. What's more, you'll be treated like a pseudo-maharaja.'

'Oh, great,' said John, lighting up. 'Don't worry about me, will you? You guys just go and have a bloody good time.'

'I told you I wouldn't be the first one off the island!' I said.

To his credit, John laughed.

However, we never made it to Orchha: nothing ever goes to plan in India. Despite Reece's enthusiasm, India's best-kept secret would have to stay that way. Our trip was once more about to be tipped on its head, this time due to the F-word.

EIGHT

A NEW F-WORD

ext morning, Brendon and I sat in the hotel foyer proudly wearing our half-pants. Reece soon joined us and shook his head ruefully. 'Where's your respect, wallahs!' he asked.

'Where's your blanket?' I replied.

'You might as well be wearing underpants! And it's cold out.'

'We're not wearing them because it's warm,' said Brendon. 'We're wearing them to piss you off.'

'Charming,' said Reece.

We had decided that this morning we would watch the sunrise on the shore of the Ganges. I could easily have stayed in bed, but my team mates had other ideas. We didn't, however, disturb John. With a hellish few weeks approaching we figured he'd much rather visit the toilet in his hotel room than the one at the end of a hectic taxi ride. Speaking of which, if you need to get to a business meeting on time in Varanasi, leave at 6.30 am. Your only hold-up will be the odd lost cow and a bunch of men carrying their dead relative on a bamboo stretcher to the river chanting, 'Ram nam satya hai' ('The name of God is the truth'). Even in death, vibrant colours are chosen: the stretcher is covered in faux gold-edged, red nylon cloth, while the corpse is wrapped in white khaddi (homespun cotton) or silk for the wealthier deceased.

Compared with the night before, the Ganges was a different being. The calming sunset was replaced by a morbid, graveyard-like fog. It was cold, creepy, uninviting.

Reece's latest flashback hardly helped. 'One day when I was here,' he said, readjusting his blanket, 'a small crowd gathered around a guy who was lying face down in the water, a couple of metres from the riverbank. The crowd grew and so did their curiosity. I decided to join them. After all, if there's a crowd in India, something is going on. Anyway, an elder soon came along and prodded the guy in the river with a long bamboo pole. His thinking being, if he's dead we need to push him downstream.'

'I can see why you like this place, Reece,' said Stew.

'Then what happened?' I asked.

'Well,' continued Reece with another hair-raising grin, 'everyone stood around the floating body for twenty minutes arguing about how they should get rid of it, when suddenly it jumped out of the water!'

'Who, the dead guy?' Brendon asked.

'He wasn't dead,' laughed Reece.

'What do you mean, he wasn't dead?' I said. 'He'd been under the water for twenty minutes. What was he, a fish?'

'Not quite. But he was a sadhu, proficient in the teachings of yoga. It's a well-known fact that some people who practise can breathe underwater for an unusually long time.'

'Yeah, but twenty minutes!' said Brendon.

'This guy had been there at least twenty minutes,' said Reece. 'I'd been watching from my balcony for ten before I even went down.'

'What did everyone do when he jumped out of the water?' Stew asked.

'They screamed and took off. You know how superstitious Indians are. And when they'd all gone, the sadhu went back under.'

As we began to walk toward one of the main funeral pyres, its piles of firewood not destined for home cooking, I thought back to the baby being dissected by wild dogs; and the cow trampling the puppy; and the exploding skulls; and stepping on a torso while having your morning dip; and seeing a miracle right in front of your eyes in the form of a sadhu who scared the shit out of innocent bystanders just for the hell of it. 'You must hate life in New Zealand, Reece.'

'It's definitely not as interesting as here.'

No one knew if we were allowed backstage at the funeral pyre, but obviously it wasn't entirely forbidden as a guide who 'didn't want money', but added, 'It's all about karma if you don't', took us under his wing. We felt voyeuristic walking down the steps to the latest body-burning where, thankfully, photography wasn't permitted. There was the son of the deceased, dressed in a white silk robe, representing purity, with his head shaved but for a tuft on top. There is some esoteric belief (especially strong among Sikhs, who never cut their hair) that hair is like a radio antenna to God. By shaving it off, the eldest son temporarily cuts his communication with the heavens, the thinking being that God can then concentrate on the soul of the deceased which, of course, is released from the body once the skull has exploded.

A sacred fire is lit in the earthen pot, and the body, after it is washed and bound about the waist with a piece of cloth, is stretched upon the bier and completely covered save the face, which is left exposed. Friends then carry away the bier. The son, who lights the funeral pyre, walks ahead with the earthen pot in his hands. When the body has been placed upon the pile, some of the mourners scatter pieces of sandalwood over the body. The chief mourner then walks around the pile three times and fires it up.

What surprised me most was that it didn't seem to concern the son in the slightest that we were effectively gatecrashing his father's funeral. You forget, too, how long it takes to burn something as dense as a corpse. Or how boring it would be. In the time we were there, no longer than ten minutes, the son made phone calls on his mobile phone, facing the water, not his father, either to escape the noise or to get a better reception. You can hardly blame him. Given that the average body takes about three hours to become ash, it must be an exhausting experience. Once it's all over, the fire is put out and all attendees proceed to the river to bathe.

Ambling up the jagged steps, we passed mounds of black hair lying on the ground. Before I knew the ins and outs of cremation, I had presumed they were the leftovers of a makeshift barber — just as I presumed my shoulders were covered in dandruff, until I realised it was probably the remains of Grandpa Singh. In fact, white flaky ash covered most of our clothing. Outside, every spare inch of space was taken up by endless stacks of firewood: two hundred kilos for part-cremation, three hundred for full.

Our 'guide' kept repeating that he didn't want a tip but to 'pay one of the widows waiting to die'. He took us to a dank upstairs room with a view of the Ganges, where three sunken-faced widows wore white saris and miserable frowns. This was the 'Death House', where the sick and old with no family were left to die. This was clearly our guide's finale, an opportunity to milk near-death for tips.

'I don't expect anything,' he repeated tirelessly. 'But it is all about karma. If you are going to give money, give to the widows.'

I caved in and gave a hundred rupees to a woman who looked as though she had only hours left. If I had known the language, I would have told her to make a run for it, because I knew exactly where the money would be going. Karma Man nodded his head and guided us down the steps, away from the widow waving weakly, death in her yellow eyes.

t breakfast in the hotel we discovered John already seated, slurping coffee. He'd been on the phone all night. Mr Straya and his wife were seated at the next table. Eager to hear stories from our trip rather than about his wife's shoe-shopping escapades, he asked how many games we had managed to play.

'Five,' said Stew, spreading another dollop of honey on his toast.

'Five, well done!' said Mr Straya. 'And how many have you won?'

'It's three-two to India,' I replied.

'Oh!' he said, rubbing his hands together. 'Close series. You'll have to bring in the big guns soon. Maybe you need a few Aussies on your team.'

Our enterprising friend, who hand-delivered candles to our boat with the expertise of an Olympic rower.

'That would be helpful,' said Stew. 'Considering we couldn't chase down a score of four in Darjeeling.'

'It was a tough pitch,' I said.

'They were eight,' Brendon replied.

Mr Straya laughed and said he wished he wasn't going shoe-shopping after breakfast.

With a few hours to fill before John flew to Cairo we took Vicky behind the hotel's bike sheds. A large open field with a 'Beware of snakes' sign became our makeshift pitch for only our second practice of the tour. We managed to convince a hotel worker to join us. The last thing we wanted was to see him fired, but we needed new blood — a fresh bowler with a tricky action and unpredictable tactics. Sadly, this player wasn't to be it. Although he batted like a blindfolded toddler and peered over his shoulder for his boss more than at the ball, it seemed to make his day. Once we had distributed his left-arm dibbly-dobblies all over the park, we allowed him to resume his duties.

And then there were four. Never in a million years did we think it would end like this, with John standing alongside the Goldfish Bowl, waving, smiling, agonising. It was only natural that he would be jealous. He had been having as great a time as the rest of us. The best time of his life had now turned to the worst. We waved. He waved. And we parted ways in the City of Death and Misery and Life. Varanasi, no longer a legend from a dusty school atlas, now harboured smells, feelings and consternation. I can't rule out ever going back. John, however, would be forgiven for taking to the damn place with an industrial strength blowtorch, his second cousin dousing and defending the city behind him.

The drive to the airport was short, even pleasant. Maybe we didn't realise how eager we were to get out of Bad Luck Town. And although it seemed technically impossible, Wasim's trousers were actually tighter than two days previous. As he walked towards the airport terminal with us in tow, I wondered how half-pants could be more offensive than a pair of slacks from *CHiPs*. It was as if Rod Stewart's Indian half-brother had thrown in his music career for one of getting Kiwis into the biggest travel mess of the century. Okay, that's not entirely fair. It wasn't all his fault, but you've got to blame someone. And today, Wasim was it.

Before the trip began, the only F-word that came out of Stew's mouth was a profanity directed at touts. But now a new noun had emerged: 'fog'. It's widely recognised that while Delhi is world-class when it comes to international flights, as far as domestic ones go it may as well be Papua New Guinea. The problem is one of technical equipment. They have the fog-landing equipment necessary for the big birds, but not for the 737s carrying the olds from Thiruvananthapuram. As a result, fog throws the country's second-largest airport (after Mumbai) into complete disarray. It's an annual affair, sending holidaymakers and business folk into a tailspin.

And it can go on for days.

Our plane was supposedly arriving from Delhi, ultimately taking us to Khajuraho, whence we would then drive to Orchha. 'India's best-kept secret' Orchha. 'Unlike anything you've ever seen' Orchha. 'You're going to love Orchha' Orchha. However, if there was no such plane leaving Delhi, then there was no plane to take us to said paradise.

Wasim fussed about as we waited in the terminal, endeavouring to make our non-journey a smooth one. Every ten minutes he would join us. 'Still fog?' we'd ask.

'Yes,' he'd reply.

'Will be leaving soon?'

'Yes, the fog will clear.'

'What if it doesn't?'

'We will arrange another flight.'

'So there are other flights?'

'No, just one flight, but the fog should clear.'

'What if it doesn't?'

'We will arrange another flight.'

'Still fog?'

'Yes . . .'

Etcetera, etcetera.

Eventually, after we had waited for two hours, the fog in Delhi became so dire that our flight was cancelled. Wasim had vanished, perhaps to buy a tight shirt to match his pants. Then a less caustic mood prevailed, and we agreed that he was probably doing his best to help we petulant Westerners. Foreigners harrumphed,

moaned and sweated. We had to make a decision, and fast. Would we get a new flight from Varanasi to Delhi and then get the train to Orchha the next day, and so have only one afternoon in such a magical place? Or would swapping plans completely mess up the remainder of the trip? More realistically, should we flag Orchha altogether and spend an extra few days in Delhi before heading to Agra, as per the itinerary?

'We don't want to spend any more time in Delhi than need be,' said Reece.

'I agree,' I said.

'Let's just bite the bullet,' said Reece, 'and take the first available flight to Delhi tonight, then take the first train tomorrow morning to India's best-kept secret?'

'Okay,' said Stew.

'Whatever,' said I.

'I think I need a loo,' said Brendon.

We felt slightly better having made a decision. But the joy was short-lived. Wasim now stood before us adjusting his crotch and grinning from ear to ear. 'Good news,' he said, handing out airline tickets. 'I've secured the last four seats for the next flight to Delhi.'

'That is good news, gee!' beamed Reece. 'We'll get to Orchha after all.'

Wasim's grin faded.

'What?' asked Reece, suspiciously.

'I just called my travel agent in Delhi,' said Wasim. 'He said there are no tickets left for the train from Delhi to Orchha tomorrow morning.'

So as it turned out, our minds had been made up for us. Tread water and move in some direction, even if it turns out to be the wrong one.

'But Orchha!' cried Reece. 'You would have loved it! It's India's —'

'Best-kept secret,' I said. 'Yes, we know.'

'Look,' said Stew, raising his voice above those of the other tetchy travellers. 'Let's just get to Delhi, have a shower and a feed, and then reassess the trip.'

'Stew's right,' said Brendon. 'Hey, at least things can't get any worse.'

But then they did. As he casually rummaged about in his daypack, he fished out a bulging leather wallet which, by its sheer size and weight, could only belong to one person. 'Oh shit,' he whispered.

I leaned in and took a closer look. 'That's . . . isn't that John's wallet?'

Brendon nodded.

'Shit,' I said.

'Shit,' said Reece.

'Fuck,' said Stew.

So now along with the new F-word we had a new problem. John's wallet was his lifeline. To say it had everything in it would be an understatement. Credit cards, frequent-flyer cards, first-class lounge cards, passport, American dollars and flight tickets stared forlornly at us like Romanian orphans. Brendon held the wallet close to his chest. The rest of us resembled onlookers at a car crash. John, no doubt blissfully unaware, was a forty-five-minute taxi ride away. In an hour, he, too, would be due at Varanasi airport for his connecting flight to Vienna and Cairo. And we had his wallet.

The problem with one of us becoming a Wallet Carrier Pigeon was that it could lead to more strife if we were to cross paths with John without knowing it. With our flight still delayed, one of us could make it back to the hotel. But what if John left at the same time?

Finally, the farmer saw some sense. A few feet from us, border patrol guards were busy sealing checked-in bags with plastic ties from an automatic machine. The result was a conundrum MacGyver would have had trouble hacking. Without hesitation, Stew marched over with John's wallet, returning with it completely bound in white plastic.

'That should do the trick,' he said. 'Now we need someone to take it to him.'

As luck would have it, the man to sort that job was standing nearby with his elegant shoe-loving wife. Once again, his choice of clothing put the Kiwi backpackers to shame: designer sports jacket, crisp white shirt, polished shoes and neatly pressed jeans. (I still haven't learned you don't have to look like a hobo when you travel.)

'Gidday fellas,' he said, smiling. 'How's everything garn?'

'Not too good actually, mate,' I said, explaining our predicament.

'Struth,' he said. 'And he's still back in the hotel, this John?'

'Yep,' said Reece.

'And you guys are about to leave?'

'We just got the last four seats to Delhi,' said Brendon.

One thing about successful people is they get things done. Some schmooze. Others grease. Mr Straya had a far more direct tactic. Having discovered Wasim was our go-to man, he cornered him, dangling the wallet like a carrot. 'Do you know this Mr John?'

Wasim looked at us. We nodded eagerly.

'Yes,' said Wasim.

'Good,' said Mr Straya. 'This is Mr John's wallet. I need you to take it directly to him. Do not go anywhere else on the way. Do you understand?'

'Yes, sir.'

'Right,' said Mr Straya, passing the wallet to Wasim. 'Cos if you don't, I'll fucking kill ya!'

Wasim gulped like a trapped rabbit. 'Kill me?' he asked meekly.

'Yes,' continued Mr Straya, as serious as a heart attack. 'Kill you.'

The contents of John's wallet could have fed and clothed Wasim's family for a year, but the risk of stealing it wouldn't be worth it. To become a tour guide in India is to win the lottery. Bribery, corruption and luck are needed. To throw that away would be suicide. Plus, the wallet was tightly bound, and although I'm probably naive I think sometimes you've just got to trust someone.

The wait was over. A new plane was about to arrive. Grumpiness and irritability ensued. Yet even when laughter is the last thing on your mind, India manages to pull one out of the bag:

The following items are not to be carried in hand luggage:
Any type of cosmetics
Lipsticks and nail polish
Liquid items, sprays
Gels, perfumes, deos
Toothpaste
Pickles

'Pickles? Why pick on the pickles?' I asked Reece once we were settled into our seats.

'They're not pickles as you and I know them,' he replied. 'Indian pickles are salty, briny, spicy preserves of lime and mango. And they stink to high heaven.'

'Poor pickles.'

'Poor us, more like,' said Reece. 'We have nowhere to stay in Delhi and we miss out on Orchha. Honestly, you don't know what you're missing.'

'And we never will,' I replied, opening page 535 of *Shantaram*.

Stew leaned over and closed his magazine. 'Are you still reading that fucking thing?' he asked.

'Sadly, yes.'

Before the pilot told us to turn off our phones, one of ours beeped.

    FROM JOHN BOUGEN:
    GOT IT, THANKS.

Wasim would live to see another day.

NINE

Previous page: Three bricks for a wicket and the obligatory shoe to denote
wide balls. Belar Road, Old Delhi.

TOO BUSY FOR CRICKET

The most memorable thing about Delhi for me is that their Chief Minister's name is Sheila Dikshit. Another far more forgettable image is of yours truly saving his stomach woes for Asia's stomach-woe capital.

Delhi Belly in Delhi. It sounds like a joke, but it wasn't. Clearly a hangover from a meal in Varanasi, an unknown force had convinced my innards to revolt, retreat and repel. Along with cramps came the uncomfortable thought that my sweatshirt was still covered in dead people's ashes. The stirrings started as we landed in Delhi. A delicious five-star curry on the plane didn't help. My first reaction to those uncomfortable rumblings, however, was much like when you hear a dodgy sound in your car's engine: just keep driving and hope it'll disappear.

Eat the curry and you won't feel like death. Wrong. Eat the curry and enhance your feeling of death.

'Finally, I've got company,' said Brendon. 'I was getting lonely there for a while.'

'Mmm,' I groaned. 'Pleased to help.'

The only problem was, Brendon had been fleecing supplies from my first-aid kit ever since his had run out in Darjeeling. Isn't it funny how, before a journey, fifty dollars for a bunch of oddly-named pills can seem a complete rip-off? You feel differently about it the day you manage to make the inside of a toilet bowl look like a Jackson Pollock painting.

Arriving late at night with no accommodation booked, the Black Craps were fractious and weary. It had been a long few days. Knowing that Orchha was no longer on the cards didn't help. Although it was nearly midnight, traffic in Delhi was still thick. In a healthier state of mind I might have smiled at the Hindus selling Santa hats at every set of traffic lights. As it was, I thought they looked ridiculous.

'Hindus don't even celebrate Christmas,' I said.

'Gee, you really have lost your sense of humour,' said Reece.

'Mmm,' I moaned.

'Where are we staying?' Brendon asked as the Goldfish Bowl edged forward.

'The Connaught,' said Reece. 'I have no idea where it is and what it's like. We booked at the last minute, so let's just hope it's close to town.'

'Does it have toilets?' I asked.

'Oh boy,' said Brendon. 'You are bad. Welcome to my world!'

'Think we'll find a nice hot vindaloo tonight,' said Reece.

'With lots of chilli!' added Stew.

'He'll be shitting through the eye of a needle in no time.'

'Hope there are some matches in the toilet.'

'That's if he makes it that far.'

'I fell into a burning ring of fire.'

It had begun.

The Connaught was a perfectly respectable hotel, if a little drab and lifeless. We should have been thankful given that we had secured such a late booking, but we couldn't get past the fact that compared to other places we'd seen, this joint seemed to have been designed by Stevie Wonder. You can tell a lot about a hotel by the guests in its foyer, and these ones looked the way I felt.

'Let's eat,' said Reece.

'Good idea, Blanket Boy,' said Stew.

'I'll meet you there,' I said, heading for the men's.

'Oo!' said Brendon, rubbing his hands together. 'I shouldn't laugh, but . . .'

'Yes you should,' said Reece.

The restaurant's soundtrack was Cliff Richard songs performed on pan flute — on repeat. That in itself would be cause to throw up a thousand times over; coupled with whatever I had picked up in the City of Misery and Death, it tipped me over the edge. To our right sat a red-faced little man from Newcastle, with glasses so thick they made his eyes look like those of a giant squid. He nursed a huge glass of beer while his non-drinking wife eavesdropped and smiled. Normally I would say hello in such a situation, especially when travelling, but

tonight I didn't trust my arse or my mouth.

A discarded ball at Belar Road, Old Delhi.

The meals arrived, looking worse than what I used to cook in my flat. No one could tell where the garish tablecloth ended and Reece's rainbow pasta began. Brendon's spaghetti looked like something from the art corner of a kindergarten. Despite this, Stew dived into his like a starved pig at a trough. These were TV dinners minus the taste.

I pushed my hot chips away; Reece pounced. 'God, you must really be sick,' he said, throwing a few in his gob.

Next, my fears were realised: our British mate wanted to talk. 'You Kiwis, are you?' he asked, with a mouthful of food.

'That's right,' said Stew.

Judging by what he said next, I can only assume he'd heard us abuse the hotel's décor, food, service and music.

'You like a bit of sledging, don't you, you Kiwis?'

'Oh yeah,' said Stew. 'We give as good as we get, especially when we play against the Poms.'

He continued to stare at us, obviously bored with his wife, and keen to join the four idiots at the table opposite. 'Your mate doesn't look very well,' he said.

Just looking at this man made me want to be sick. It was something about the way his food fell out of his mouth as he ate, the way his gut hung out of his tight T-shirt, the way his man-boobs put his wife's to shame. But mostly it was because what I really needed now was Keira Knightley and Alicia Keys dressed as nurses, not Benny Hill's fatter, sweatier, less funny brother.

'He's got a bit of Delhi Belly,' said Reece, scraping the leftover sauce from his plate and licking his knife.

'That's irony for you!' said the Pom. 'Delhi Belly — in Delhi!'

'Mmm,' I said.

'You going to be sick?' pressed the Pom.

'Eventually,' I said, and left the table with exactly that intention.

eeing Delhi after dark was postponed due to the late hour. Sometimes a bed beats pretty much anything. We shuffled into the hotel lift, where an Indian guest saw our scuffed cricket bat. (Why we had taken it to dinner was anyone's guess — maybe we thought we could get a game in between mains and dessert.)

'Cricket?' he asked.

'Yes,' said Brendon.

'Where?'

'In the streets, mainly,' said Stew.

The Indian man paused momentarily, seeming unsure what to say next. Then he saw my Black Caps hat.

'From New Zealand?'

'That's right,' said Reece.

'You know Lou Vincent?'

'Yes,' we replied, thinking of the Auckland and New Zealand player known for his big-hitting, crowd-pleasing style.

'Very ugly,' said the Indian man, as if chewing on a wasp.

Awkward silence as we watched the floor numbers change. Mr Honest said no more.

'This is our stop,' said Stew at last, and we headed for shut-eye.

Reece, as well as being the New Slush Fund Boss, was also Stew's new room-mate. Brendon and I were quietly thankful that we had managed to evict our unrelenting sleep thief. Swapping one snorer for another ensured that Stew's ear plugs were still the most-used item in his backpack. Our room was like a scene from *The Odd Couple*, with Brendon's belching and gas-induced performances topped only by my multiple visits to a toilet three metres from his bed. The night was made complete for me when my big toenail — which had had a laptop fall on it a week before departure, remember? — finally fell off.

'Should I keep it as a memento?' I asked Brendon before turning out the light.

'That is just disgusting!' he replied, turning to face the wall.

'I'll take that as a no.'

'Very perceptive.'

ypical that the hardened farmer should never get sick, but at least he had an extensive first-aid kit. The next morning, with my stomach cramps in full flight, I flogged some of Stew's Buscopan pills as he devoured CNN. I stole his remote control too. Every other channel was cricket, which we hardly minded, but it was the Indian commercials that really made our morning. Funny how watching ads at home is a chore, yet when visiting foreign climes they become an event.

First product: a mosquito repellent ridding your home of not only itchy bites but also dengue fever and malaria.

Second product: Mass, a powdered drink which makes women, wait for it, get bigger. 'Are you having trouble putting on weight — and keeping it on? Wait no longer. Mass will help you gain those pounds — and keep them on!'

The Connaught's business centre was no place to do business, but at least it had email. First, I had to get a password for the computer. The man who took my money was an Indian version of Doctor Bunsen Honeydew from *The Muppet Show*. Sharpening his pencil, he glanced at my name on the hotel form, paused, then looked up at me with a pert grin. 'But Mr Brown,' he said. 'You are white.'

I was still laughing when I reached the others in reception, where a grimacing Stew, pacing in a circular motion, covered his ears. 'Aargh!' he said. 'Make it stop! They're still playing Cliff Richard!'

The same CD, seemingly the only CD the Connaught owned, spewed through the overhead speakers, ensuring that 'Devil Woman' and 'Summer Holiday' polluted our heads until nightfall. The English bloke from the previous evening approached with his wife. He took one look at me and remarked to the others, 'I was thinking, your sick mate here needs some bike clips for his pants.'

'Why's that?' asked Stew.

'To keep the shit in.'

I would have laughed if I wasn't busy trying not to vomit.

As we hit the streets of Delhi, we discussed two things we hadn't seen in India: parking wardens and children's car seats. The former are something most civilised places could do without. The latter is a multimillion-dollar industry which somehow convinces every parent that their car will crash at some stage and their baby will be in it. Cars collide, sure, and any parent with half a brain wouldn't hesitate to buckle their child in, but as we watched whole families ride past on mopeds, babies included, it made us wonder whether our Western heightened paranoia did anybody any good.

Delhi is divided into the old and the new. New Delhi, built as the imperial capital by the British, is open and planned; vibrant Old Delhi served as the capital of Islamic India. As with any destination, however, one's view is tarnished (or enhanced) by previous experiences. Reece used to live here, and it reminded

Above: Anshul (on the right) proudly wears his Man of the Match cap, which would later be stolen by the school bully.

Left: If we had a rupee for every time we saw Reece in this situation ...

him of work. I had been to Delhi once before, for forty-eight hours in similar temperatures, doing my best — as every know-it-all backpacker does — to 'get off the beaten track and find the real India'. The result was a frustrating stay, most of which was spent at Delhi railway station, sweating and arguing with pushy women and freedom fighters, those who have at one time or another fought for India's sovereignty. I also remember a two-star hotel's toilet spewing its contents everywhere, after naively thinking that the flush button would do just that. Delhi also provided me with my first taste of terrorism. Hand-painted on my seat on a rickety bus was a sign: 'Look under your seat. There could be a bomb. Raise alarm. Earn reward.'

Delhi is hardly a reason to come to India. Like most major cities, it's the stepping stone to something more memorable. With that in mind, two days in a city we weren't enamoured with was going to be hard work. Then again, maybe it would surprise us. I guess Delhi just reminded us that we should have been in Orchha.

'Reece,' I said, 'for the love of God, would you stop going on about Orchha.'

'But we'd be there by now.'

'Let it go, Blanket Boy,' said Stew.

Despite there being a slew of emphysema-inducing taxis available, today's plan was to try out Delhi's metro system, which has been operational since 2002, with sixty-two stations and three lines. The concept was dreamed up in 1960 and work finally began in 1995. Leaving India behind, we rode the escalators down underground to what could easily have been Ealing Broadway or Baker Street. (In fact, if you ever lose it above ground in Delhi, grab a Coke and go below — the metro is quiet, spotless and relaxing.) At the entrances, a line of beggars was being whipped by a trigger-happy guard. It achieved nothing, of course: like a tide, the beggars returned as soon as the guard turned his back. Before embarking, we were searched — as was everyone — and then took our place on an empty

carriage underneath India's capital, passing a billboard for one of the metro's newest cafes: Piccadelhi.

As we left the metro building, a rare sight greeted us: blue sky. One of the conditions for securing the 2010 Commonwealth Games was Delhi's skies had to be cleared of smog. Consequently, every auto-rickshaw (and there are only a few million of them) had to be converted to CNG if they wanted to stay on the road. Trucks, too, were allowed to enter the city only between midnight and 6 am. It has made a difference — the Smurf-blue sky was as clear as anything we had seen in pollution-free Darjeeling.

The beeping, however, seemed — impossibly — even louder than in Kolkata. On the roads there were no lanes, just a mass of bikes and rickshaws and taxi drivers. No order either, just fit in where you can. In the middle of this chaos, tireless workers transported flour, bamboo, bananas, peanuts, buckets and customers on antiquated transport. A mother, snotty-nosed toddlers by her side, stood in the middle of the road adjusting her sari while trucks carrying white goats with brown socks patiently steered around her.

Nearby, a guide's eyes lit up as he spotted the four remaining Black Craps. Convinced he was onto a winner, he ambled beside us, full of bravado. 'You want to see Old Delhi?' he inquired.

'No thanks,' Brendon replied, speeding up so as to keep warm.

'The Red Fort?'

'No.'

'Great Mosque?'

'Not today.'

'Humayun's Tomb?'

'No thanks,' said Stew, swinging the bat. 'We just want a game of cricket.'

Finding such a game in Delhi was not going to be an issue given the enthusiasm shown by more than a dozen local school kids in ties and blazers who ran over to us. Their excitement was at fever pitch. 'Cricket! Cricket!'

'I'll bowl!'

'Please, sir, give me bat!'

'We play! We play!'

Like it or not, it was game on with Jain Sanskrit Community School.

'Please come,' said the chubby ringleader, scurrying toward an inner-city park where businessmen sat on ramshackle benches eating their lunch amid long grass, rubbish and cow dung. The boys rolled their sleeves up and began building wickets from bricks, while others took turns at hurling Vicky towards Stew.

'OK!' he said. 'Let's get a proper game going.' And we were back into it. The familiar crowd enveloped Blanket Boy and his scorebook. Brendon took his camera from his bag, and I prayed that the 'blockers' I had taken one hour earlier

were going to work.

But before that first ball was even bowled, a policeman in his late seventies drew a halt to proceedings. Whether Granddad was still in the force or whether he had scored his uniform from a fancy-dress shop was debatable, but the schoolboys seemed to take his demands seriously. Despite being kids, they were local and, by default, our only guide. Plus, Granddad had a baton. Then again, we had a cricket bat.

Probably the truest pitch we played on (concrete's good that way). Belar Road, Old Delhi.

It was time for a little negotiation. 'Just a quick game, OK?' I asked.

'No cricket!' said the policeman, shooing the boys away like seagulls from chips.

'But we won't be long,' I persisted.

Blank face. Don't mess with me. I could go and hire an Indian Army outfit. 'No cricket,' he repeated.

'But we've come all the way from New Zealand.'

'No cricket.'

'Please convince him,' pleaded the Chubster, hands in the prayer position. 'Please convince him.'

But Granddad was in no mood for compromise. Not that he needed to be. Within seconds of the match being called off, the boys fled like robbers in the night. We could just make out their petrified faces as they hid behind a nearby bush. 'Teacher's coming!' they hissed in unison.

Detention averted, the boys dragged us to a barely open gate by one of Delhi's town halls. What greeted us was a concrete coliseum, complete with a four-metre cast-iron fence to prevent stray sixes. A few stray layabouts smoking bidis by the town hall's steps attempted to thwart our plans, but such a perfect setting demanded action. One abandoned game was as much as we could stomach. We needed to get the tour back on track, as our last game had been on that awful day in Varanasi.

'What's the series score again?' I asked Stew, marking my run up.

'Three–two to India,' he replied.

'No pressure, then.'

Intense concentration as the Belar Road XI try to knock over the Black Craps.

And none was felt. For once we had India on the ropes, my 'blockers' convincing my bowling arm that putting the ball on the stumps actually gets results. Suddenly, we had the Jain Sanskrit Community School five for two and looking shakier by the minute.

Then, as if he had a direct line to Granddad himself, the manager of the town hall shuffled and spluttered his way towards us. He was a big unit, and the process of his joy-killing probably meant pushing his body to places it hadn't been since Ganguly was a nipper. We didn't need to know Hindi — we could tell what was coming from the look on his face.

'Sorry, fellas,' said Reece, after a brief discussion with Red Tape Guy. 'We're not allowed to play here. The manager's just informed me the match is abandoned.'

'Tell him we just came from an abandoned match!' I said.

Blanket Boy smiled. 'You tell him.'

'We don't speak Hindi,' Brendon said.

'At least ask him if we can finish,' said Stew.

We watched as Blanket Boy smiled like a drunk and spoke a language which still made us laugh every time we heard him speak it. Red Tape Guy's reaction, a stern shake of the head, was not promising. And so it was that the second game in ten minutes was called off thanks to the Indian Fun Police.

The boys from Jain Sanskrit didn't take the abrupt ending well. Once again, the

Chubster tapped my shoulder. 'Please convince him,' he implored. I told him we had tried our best. I could see the disappointment in his eyes. It's only a game, sure, but he and his mates were obviously keen to have a go at the Kiwis. Plus, it was better than going to calculus.

If we couldn't play, the least I could do was interview their Man of the Match, sixteen-year-old Salam Mohammed. 'Favourite players?' I asked, opening my note-book.

'Tendulkar and Ricky Ponting,' he grinned.

I looked to the Black Craps. 'Same answer every time.'

'Never a Kiwi,' added Stew.

'Family?'

'Two sisters, two brothers.'

'Favourite subject?'

'Computers. I want to be a com-'

'-puter engineer,' I said finishing his sentence. 'You wouldn't be the first in India. Favourite film?'

'*Dhoom.*'

'Favourite singer?'

The answer, Himesh, was an artist the rest of the boys laughed at. Maybe because nothing is cool, even the cool stuff, when you're a teenager. (Himesh Reshammiya, a Bollywood composer, singer and actor, is a pretty big deal, and was the first Indian star to perform at London's Wembley Stadium.)

We presented Salam with an Auckland Aces cap and started to head to wherever the next abandonment lay. I still felt like a bag of arseholes, but when you're travelling even the worst days are better than Mondays at home. As the boys moped off, Reece, who up until now had been loitering around the town hall, joined us. 'The man who just ruined our game wants us to join him for tea.'

Such is India. It was hard to believe that Mr Hansraj Sharma was the same guy who had rained on our parade. Stoically proud of his town hall, which looked no better on the inside than out, he gave us a short tour of his workplace. It was cold, dark and concrete. I couldn't imagine a performance in such an uninspiring venue.

'Very busy!' said Mr Sharma, showing us another empty area. 'That's why you mustn't play cricket.'

'Not too busy today,' said Stew, his voice echoing through the chamber.

'Very busy!' he continued. 'Ceremonies, functions, weddings!'

He showed us two bride rooms then offered tea, which we declined in favour of finding a game of cricket which would last longer than a Bob Dylan song.

Game abandoned; a shame because we had Jain Sanskrit Community in tatters. Stew clearly wants a third opinion; I clearly need some dress sense.

TOWN HALL, OLD DELHI, DELHI

INDIA

Rahul (15) bowled Salman 0
Sumit (15) caught Justin 2
Vivek (15) bowled Justin 0

BOWLING

Milan (16) 1-3, Justin 2-2

MATCH ABANDONED DUE TO UNCO–OPERATIVE TOWN HALL MANAGEMENT (TOO BUSY — YEAH RIGHT).

TEN

Previous page: The only difference between life and death in India is a rickshaw ride. But what fun!

COWBOYS IN INDIA

Like any red-blooded male, I've taken part in my fair share of cowboys and Indians encounters, but never had I seen an Indian dressed as a cowboy until we sat down to eat at Rodeo, a Mexican restaurant that served margaritas and non-stop country music in Delhi's commercial centre. As our big-grinned waiter, resplendent in cowboy hat, bandana, boots and holster passed us menus, Stew and I thanked our lucky stars that Cliff Richard was nowhere to be heard. But Wham! were. And so was Chris de Burgh. 'Lady in Red' filtered through the overhead speakers as we set about ordering Mexican food in an Indian city. Brendon, still a casualty, took his slowly. I ordered and again, to Reece's great pleasure, passed my plate to him as soon as I saw it.

'She's an interesting place, I'll give it that,' said Stew, alluding to Delhi and all her quirks. Having walked, taxied and bluffed our way around the city centre, where people nagged, touched, pulled and prodded, we'd finally decided on the most Western place we could find.

Maybe we were going soft.

'Used to have some great piss-ups here,' said Reece, looking over at the mock-saddle seats at the bar. 'We used to come and sing karaoke after work.'

'Hold me back,' I said, now tolerating Wham!'s 'Last Christmas', which actually comforted me in a funny sort of way.

'I'm just glad to be out of Very-Nasty,' said Stew.

'You guys didn't even see the place,' said Reece. 'Try living there.'

'No thanks,' said Brendon. 'We'll leave that up to you.'

'Next time we go to Very-Nasty I'll enrol you on the six-month yoga course I did back in 1991,' said Reece, grinning like a fool.

'Something tells me it wasn't just yoga,' said Stew, sipping his lager.

'No,' said Reece. 'We also had to drink our own urine for six months.'

'What?'

Reece sat back and wallowed in nostalgia. He downed another Old Monk and cola that Brendon would be putting on his credit card. 'Indians believe that cow's urine is a good tonic. Some take it to the next extreme — your own urine is the best. Everyone on the course had to drink it.'

'For six months?' Brendon asked.

'Yep.'

'Every morning?'

'Uh-huh.'

'While it was still warm?'

'Yep.'

This, you can understand, took a while to sink in. Generally, dinner-party conversations are about house sales, school fees and politics. Being told by someone wearing a blanket that he used to drink the contents of his bladder rendered us speechless. But not for long.

'Surely,' I said, coming up for breath, 'you didn't have to drink the whole lot. I mean, some mornings you can piss for five minutes.'

'We didn't have to drink the first hundred mills.'

'Oh, right. Walk in the park then.'

'But that's the most potent part,' mused Stew. 'Darkest in colour.'

'Exactly,' said Reece. 'That's why they don't make you drink it. Look, if you have a sound diet, eat and drink all the right things, your piss should be clear and taste almost like hot water.'

If my tortillas and enchiladas seemed abhorrent before, news of Reece's past dietary disasters rendered them inedible. Blanket Boy, however, once again failed to grasp that instead of being shocked by his stories, we often wanted more.

'When you drank it,' said Brendon, as if finally tuning in to how dire Reece's past had been, 'did it actually make you feel better?'

'Not really,' replied Reece.

'Then why did you do it?'

'It was all part of the course. It was about stamina, control, diligence.'

'Fucking insanity more like,' said Stew, ordering another lager.

'Did anyone go mad?' I asked.

'Lisa, a Swiss girl, went a bit crazy. She took a bit of convincing that drinking her own piss was a good thing to do.'

'You think?'

Then the questions we really wanted answered came to the floor. 'Did you gargle?' Stew asked.

'Can we just drop it?'

'This Lisa girl, did she go nuts?'

'She was already nuts! Look, let's just . . .'

'Was she hot?'

'No, not really. She married a sadhu.'

'Did you have to drink her piss as well?'

'Stop!' cried Reece. 'Please, just stop!'

Like shooting fish, I tell you.

As we left Rodeo we were attacked once more by lepers and beggars. In a sounder frame of mind I wouldn't be so direct, but Delhi's smell of kerosene, burning plastic and coal, with a sickly-sweet aftertaste of incense and raw sewage, made me almost dry-retch. Reece, too, lost his cool when a beggar yanked his arm and didn't let go. 'Jao baseriwala!' he yelled.

And they skedaddled, quicker than lager turns to urine, which was ironic given our dinner discussion. Stunned by what we had seen, we gathered around our new hero. 'What the hell did you say to that guy?' we asked.

'Jao baseriwala.'

'Which translates to?'

'Fuck off, you homeless piece of shit.'

'That'll do it,' said Stew.

This less than typical outburst from Reece was proof that he was slowly losing it. And we were partly responsible — which made us feel very, very proud.

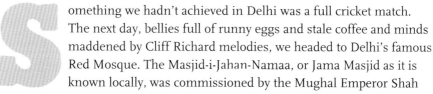omething we hadn't achieved in Delhi was a full cricket match. The next day, bellies full of runny eggs and stale coffee and minds maddened by Cliff Richard melodies, we headed to Delhi's famous Red Mosque. The Masjid-i-Jahan-Namaa, or Jama Masjid as it is known locally, was commissioned by the Mughal Emperor Shah Jahan (who also built the Taj Mahal) and completed in 1656 AD. It took five thousand workers six years to build; the courtyard alone can hold twenty-five thousand worshippers.

Due to the early hour, many of Delhi's estimated one hundred thousand homeless people were still asleep on the mosque's concrete steps. Space was at a premium, even on such an unforgiving surface. Toddlers, however, are the same the world over. When we threw one group Vicky, they put down their makeshift

bat, a jandal, and joined in. An attempt to leave, however, was thwarted by an older boy who tried to trip me up and grab my bat.

'Give me bat!' he demanded, trailing close behind.

'No.'

'Give me bat!' he hissed, this time inches from my face.

I was losing my nerve. 'No,' I said. 'Fuggoff!'

As luck would have it, we went from the most aggressive man in India to two of the most charming. Rahul and Sajeet were old pros when it came to the gift of the gab, insisting that we accompany them to a nearby park to set up a proper game. They jeered at the boy who demanded my bat and soon Stew and I were sitting on the back of Sajeet's bike, Brendon and Reece on Rahul's.

'Do you live in Delhi?' I asked Sajeet, as he started pedalling.

'Yes, we sleep at the police station.'

These boys were fantastic riders, and fit too, neither showing any sign of strain despite lugging Westerners who had a soft spot for butter and beer.

'We find you a park, and then we play,' said Sajeet.

'Righto, boss,' said Stew. 'You lead the way.'

A game of cricket, a good tip and no need to find customers the rest of the morning. No wonder the boys were smiling.

We might have had wheels instead of legs, but the hustle of Delhi was still merciless. Along with the mandatory cars, donkeys and Tata trucks were Muslim mothers on mopeds, burqas conveniently protecting them from unwanted fumes. Other women held their biker hubby's love-handles as newborns dozed on their backs. The next cycle rickshaw housed seven kids. Here were Delhi-ites wearing scarves, jackets and beanies, even though you never imagine an Indian city outside the Himalayas having a temperature in single figures.

Animated stallholders prepared jalebi, orange toffee fritters swilling in rosewater syrup; puri bhaji, big balloon pastry breads served with jeera potato curry; steaming hot samosas served with pickled chilli and mint paste; and Reece's favourite, idli, fermented rice cakes served with sweet coconut chutney. Street food like this is always served in small bowls made out of leaves, often from the peepul tree, while spoons are often fashioned out of twigs from the neem tree. The idea is that, once replete, you toss your leaf plate and neem-stick spoon on the road and a nearby holy cow mops up the remains.

What I've just explained may sound exotic, but the pile of fish on a neighbouring cart wasn't quite so inviting. 'Oh God,' I said, catching a whiff. 'I want to vomit.'

Right arm over, one to come. It wasn't only youngsters who wanted to humiliate the Black Craps. Red Mosque, Delhi.

'Smells pretty good though, Delhi,' Stew said, videoing the madness for his kids.

'Are you joking?'

'Better than Kolkata, anyway.'

'You're just lowering your standards.'

'Maybe I've lost my nose,' he admitted.

I never fail to feel guilty on rides like this. It's the same part of the brain that rebukes you for hiring a cleaner when you're more than capable of vacuuming your own floors. Here was Sajeet doing everything but die while we discussed the trivialities of life.

'Today you can watch Victoria play Tasmania live,' remarked Stew, the trip's news and sports encyclopedia. 'A domestic game from Australia, live on Indian TV. Isn't that incredible?'

An elderly gentleman lapped us, carrying a university student a quarter his age.

By the side of the road, more people slept in freezing shade amid constant yelling, chatter and horns. Scrawny dogs sunned themselves on the footpath, their paws hanging over the kerb, Sphinx-style. Their hogging the best spot reminded me of what Mark Twain had said about India: 'All life seems to be sacred except human life.'

'Who are these people?' I asked. 'And where are they going?'

Sajeet's riding technique continued to daze, a vertical line of sweat on his back the only evidence that he was exercising at all. When the going got tough, he grabbed onto the back of Rahul's bike: tricks of the trade.

'That's the way!' said an admiring Stew.

'Twenty rupees if we beat those pricks,' said Brendon to his driver upon realising what was happening.

Rahul had his mind on far more pressing affairs. 'If you don't mind,' he said, 'Sajeet and I will play cricket with you. We are six,' he said, counting us all while riding. 'We find more when we get to park.'

Guilt was soon replaced by exhilaration. But now we faced a fresh challenge: a Delhi intersection. Clearly the initial part of our journey had taken place on one the city's calmer side streets. Suddenly, bicycles like ours were a rarity; auto-rickshaws and cars were king. A massive eighteen-wheeler lounged in the crossroads like a stubborn bull. Car alarms sounded. No one moved. Yet, amid all this, drivers directed each other into impossible paths. In India, there's always a way.

Sajeet and Rahul spotted such a slight gap and entered the slipstream. 'Good luck,' Stew said to me. 'It's your side.'

Buses and over-laden trucks did everything but graze my arm as we hit the main highway. Sajeet pedalled on in a low gear. We breathed out as gusts of black smoke clouded our path. Everything in Asia with a wheel hurled towards us, only to swerve at the last second. Each vehicle seemed to take on the persona of a punter at a rock concert where someone from the back has started pushing. The result was a moving mass of misdirection.

'Ever feel like you're right in the middle of the road?' Stew asked.

'Yep,' I said, pulling my arm in. 'That's because we are.'

I prodded Reece with the cricket bat as we rode side by side.

'Bloody whities,' he yelled. 'They're everywhere!'

He didn't take the bashing well, answering in Hindi and gaining a huge laugh from our drivers. They were still doubled over by the next intersection.

'What the hell did you say to them, Blanket Boy?' I asked, once we were stationary.

'I called you a gora.'

I put on my best Indian accent, so as to be understood, and asked Sajeet what we had been labelled. He giggled, too embarrassed to reply. Reece basked in our ignorance. 'It's a derogatory term,' he said, 'meaning "white honky".'

This sent our drivers into orbit on the laughing stakes. Like kids who'd just been gifted their first whoopee cushion, we now had our first Indian joke.

'Reece,' I said. 'You gora!'

Rahul and Sajeet: 'Ha! Ha! Ha!'

'Reece, you dirty great gora!'

Rahul and Sajeet: 'HA! HA! HA!'

Ah, fresh ammo.

Rahul and Sajeet dropped us at a rambling park with purpose-built concrete blocks at evenly spaced distances, perfect for lunchtime cricket matches. The outfield consisted of tinder-dry grass and thousands of tiny white pieces of rubbish, like the leftover tissue that comes out of a trouser pocket after a spin cycle. Nearby factories spewed dark green sludge straight into an adjoining stream. Stacked bricks, five high, provided ideal stumps, their makers no doubt oblivious to what their products were best suited for.

'Let's get this show on the road,' said Stew, rubbing his hands together.

Rahul gathered schoolboys from various friendlies around the park before the toss of a ten-rupee coin mid-pitch. The boys leaned in closer as the coin took flight. 'Heads!' I called.

After a perfect arc, the coin came to a halt by Sajeet's well-worn sandal. 'Heads it is,' he said.

'We'll have a bat,' I said to the opposing captain. He nodded, spinning Vicky from hand to hand, Shane Warne-style.

'Come on, guys,' I said. 'We need this one. We're three–two down, remember?'

'Not that we're taking it seriously,' said Brendon, lying on the grass with his camera gear, the part of his job he loved most.

'Speak for yourself,' said Stew. 'We're here to win.'

'Second is first loser,' I reiterated. 'Got the scorebook ready, Blanket Boy?'

But he was lost in a sea of cricketing hopefuls, clambering to get their name in a book he would quite happily never see again.

Cricket can be a cruel game, as one of our new mates was about to discover. Rahul, who had been gagging to play, having ridden halfway across Delhi in a feverish fervour to do so, was clean-bowled second ball. We all felt for him. It was only a social game, but everyone likes to impress.

Then Delhi provided us with our first pitch invader, in the form of a fat bully in a tight T-shirt who clearly terrorised his school mates on a daily basis. He was aggressive and ugly, snatching the bat from whoever was playing and proceeding to whack the next delivery halfway to Pakistan. His younger counterparts were particularly obliging, cowering whenever he approached.

'Twat,' we muttered.

Each time Bully Boy did this, the perfectly mannered Anshul ran to fetch the ball. He never complained and he always smiled. And I ended up batting with him. He must have had a positive effect, because for the first time I saw Vicky like a watermelon. It could have been that the pitch was even concrete, making Vicky's consistency that of an oversized bouncy ball, but I'll bank the sixteen not out. Anshul went on to make a masterful thirty-five, pounding Vicky to all parts of the ground. Couple that with retrieving the ball when Bully Boy came back for an encore, and you have a man in the making.

With sixty-seven on the board, it was Delhi's turn. As I handed the bat to the barefoot wicketkeeper, I understood the Indian tradition of placing one shoe a metre or so from the stumps, as a measurement for wides. Then their number three, Yogesh, very nearly stole the show, peppering the boundary with shots the rest of us could only dream of. Needing six off the last ball, however, he managed only four.

As I stood alone on the mid-wicket boundary, I realised that I still hadn't felt a gust of wind in India. Brendon's feats aside, of course.

Reece should be commended for completing such an accurate entry, particularly as a steady torrent of abuse was directed his way throughout. At the conclusion of the match, I asked what the cheeky jumbucks had yelled at me in Hindi as I bowled.

'You don't want to know,' he replied.

'What?' I said, offended. 'It can't be that bad. Were they heckling me?'

'They called you bahinchod about fifty times.'

'Bahinchod?' I scratched my head. 'You've used that before, doesn't it mean . . .'

'Sister fucker, yes. They repeatedly called you "sister fucker" and you repeatedly smiled and nodded in return. About fifty times.'

We envied Reece's secret weapon. I was shocked, sure, but not nearly as much as our juvenile opposition, who had been swearing like troopers for the entire match. Reece dropped the bombshell when they went one step too far.

'You speak Hindi?' they squealed.

Reece's answer in the local lingo confirmed their fears.

'Shit, I mean . . . man!' said one. 'What have we been saying?'

'Oh, all sorts of things,' said a satisfied Reece, holding all the cards. If we could have bottled the looks on their faces . . .

With a win under our belts, the boys walked us back to our bikes. The Man of the Match cap was awarded to Anshul, who was seventeen and wanted to be a dentist. Unsurprisingly, his favourite cricketers were Tendulkar and Adam Gilchrist.

It took every fibre of our being not to join every game we saw. These kids were the lucky ones, protected by a three metre-high fence around Delhi's mosque.

BELAR ROAD, OLD DELHI

BLACK CRAPS

Rahul bowled Dipu 1
Samid retired 10
Justin not out 16
Anshul not out 34
Extras 6

TOTAL 67

BOWLING

Manish 0-15, Rahul 0-6, Dipu 1-4, Vishad
    0-10, Yogesh 0-13, Deepak 0-15

INDIA

Manish caught Justin 6
Rahul bowled Amul 9
Dipu bowled Rahul 2
Vishad not out 0
Yogesh not out 35
Extras 10

TOTAL 62

BOWLING

Rahul 1-11 (five no-balls!),
    Samid 0-14, Stew 1-14, Justin 1-1,
    Amul 0-11, Anshul 0-6

BLACK CRAPS WIN.
SERIES LEVEL 3–3.

'Where's your Man of the Match hat?' Stew asked him as we climbed aboard. Anshul bowed his head, ashamed to speak. 'It has been stolen.'

'Was it the bully that kept trying to ruin our game?' I asked.

'Yes, sir,' he replied.

We looked around for the bully. He was nowhere in sight. There was little we could do.

Anshul could see we weren't happy. 'Please don't worry,' he said, shaking our hands. 'Thank you for the game. It was lovely to meet you. Good luck with your travels.'

We waved goodbye, as Rahul and Sajeet manoeuvred a clean break into Delhi's web of traffic. 'Oh well,' said Stew, wiping sweat from his brow. 'He'll do better in the long run than the fuckwit who stole his hat.'

I n India the only difference between life and death is a taxi ride. With these thoughts in mind, we put our faith once more in Sajeet, who proved a magician when it came to exploiting gaps and lesser drivers' failings. His bike bell was a welcome change from the unremitting sound of car horns. As we approached our first set of lights, a beggar approached us. He had two thumbs on one hand and was wearing only one jandal. Behind him on the pavement a man, I swear, was dead. He lay in the sun, half-naked, pants halfway down his legs, flies all over his torso and backside. Apparently early-morning Delhi has someone assigned to pick up dead bodies from the streets. More often than not, these people aren't identified but are just taken directly to the crematorium.

Sajeet by now knew us well and offered to ride via Feroz Shah Kotla, where India had recently played Pakistan in an historic test. 'India win,' he said, pointing to the stadium. 'By six wickets!'

The ground is best known for Anil Kumble's ten wickets in an innings and Sunil Gavaskar's twenty-ninth test century, equalling the great Sir Donald Bradman's long-standing record.

'It's a lot smaller than on TV,' I said.

'Pardon, sir?' asked Sajeet.

'Don't worry,' said Stew. 'He's just being a smartarse.'

Reece, who hadn't so much as paid for a chapati all trip, was now handing out bills willy-nilly, but our riders deserved it. They looked beat.

'More work today?' I asked as Rahul put the notes in his pocket. 'Or rest?'

'Rest, I think,' said Sajeet.

'Yes,' puffed Rahul. 'Rest.'

And back on their bikes they hopped, heading towards Delhi police station for an afternoon siesta.

ELEVEN

Question: what sort of idiot doesn't know what a eunuch is?
Answer: this idiot.

On the five-hour ride to Agra we stopped to pay a toll, having passed through the unmemorable towns of Badarpur, Hodal and Kosi. And that's when four eunuchs rapped on our driver's window. They giggled, flirted, and strutted suggestively.

'Here we go,' said Reece, laughing.

'What?' we asked.

'Eunuchs.'

My confusion was obvious. All I knew was that the pests in question looked like extras from *The Birdcage* or *Priscilla, Queen of the Desert*.

'Never heard of eunuchs?' Reece asked.

'Never,' I said. 'Are they transvestites, prostitutes, what?'

'A eunuch is a castrated man,' said Reece. 'In India there's a whole caste of eunuchs and transgendered individuals who sing bawdy songs about other people, including their families.'

'I don't get it,' I said, watching one of the eunuchs put his lips up to the driver's window, while the other, swathed in traditional sari and heavy make-up, pouted like Marilyn Monroe. 'Why?'

'The idea is that you pay to shut them up.'

This is not something you hear in conversation and then blissfully move on. There were questions. I found out later from the Journeyman Pictures documentary *A Eunuch's Life* that there are approximately

seven hundred thousand hijras, as they're known in Hindi, in Mumbai alone. The term 'eunuch', however, is misleading, because few hijras are actually castrated. Some are born with physically indeterminate sex; others are boys who, for whatever reason, want to be girls. Hijras beg for money and, if refused, loudly curse while exposing the area between their legs where their genitals used to be. They act as prostitutes, too, for men who can't afford the price of a real woman. Of course, they're also popular with men who like transsexuals. Due to the stigma that having a hijra child creates — other children in the family will be less attractive as a marriage partner — many Indian families figure it's just better to get rid of them. They typically live on the margins of society, face discrimination and earn a living by turning up uninvited to weddings, births and new shop openings. These ceremonies are supposed to bring good luck and fertility, while the curse of an unappeased hijra is feared by many. Some Indian provincial officials have even used hijras to collect taxes in the same fashion: they knock on the doors of shopkeepers while dancing and singing, and embarrass them into paying. And their work motto? 'Pay up or we'll play up! Or even worse, sing some more!'

Our eunuchs got what they wanted: our drivers paid them to go away and we left unscathed.

Unbelievably, the remaining stretch of road to Agra was mostly free of traffic, but for the odd Tata, which typically made its Herculean presence felt metres from the Goldfish Bowl's backside. Hundreds more trucks were parked by the roadside, waiting until midnight, when they were allowed to re-enter Delhi.

Brendon, now suffering the full effects of whatever I had had a few days before, was listening to Jack Johnson on his iPod, which was a pretty good option in view of what was playing in the van. I'm all for buying music from where I visit, but Bollywood tunes can irk after a time.

'What are they singing about?' I asked Reece.

He passed me a magazine he had stolen from the plane. It said, 'Bollywood may continue to churn out conventional storylines, but the songs are marked with unbelievable creativity,' and quoted 'Batata vada' from the film *Hifazat*:

Batata vada, aye batata vada	Potato fritter, aye potato fritter
Dil nahi dena tha, dena pada	I don't want to give me heart, but had to give
Batata vada, ho batata vada,	Potato fritter, ho potato fritter
Pyar nahi karma tha, kama pada.	I didn't want to fall in love, but had to.

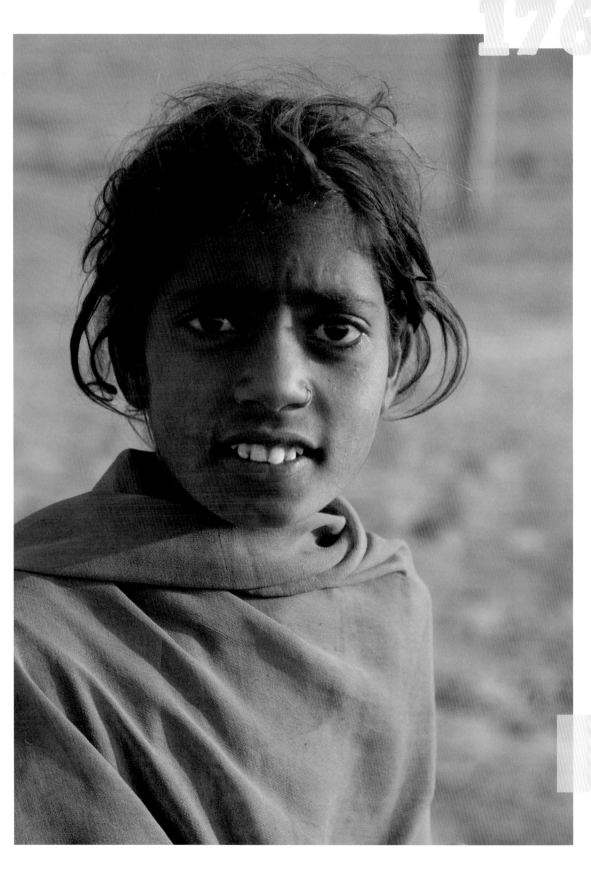

As further evidence, it quoted 'A-aa ee u-uu uu, mera dil na todo' from the film *Raja Babu*:

A-aa ee u-uu uu, mera dil na todo	A-aa ee u-uu uu, don't break my heart
Rooth ka na jao meri jaan, paas mere aao meri jaan	Don't be miffed and go my darling
Main angootha chhaap padhana aur likhana jaanoon na.	I'm illiterate, I don't know how to read and write.

Quite.

gra arrived in a flash. Soon we heard the familiar, whiny putt-putt-putt of a thousand mopeds on their last legs. Horns, dust and smoke: ah, how we had missed them over the last five hours. Most of Agra is on the west bank of the Yamuna River, with the Agra Fort and Taj Mahal at its heart. Along with its tag as the third apex of the 'golden triangle' — Delhi and Jaipur being the other two — Agra is perhaps more aptly described as a sprawling industrial city. Brick walls, brick houses, and brick factories. Bricks everywhere. I have never seen so many bricks.

Our hotel boasted Agra's only view of the Taj Mahal. From our window, four floors up, we looked down on the city with complacency and happiness, knowing the van trip was behind us and the afternoon ours. I taped the sound of the horns on my mobile, concerned that I would forget the noise we loved to hate. Brendon couldn't wait to get clicking. Against a peach-pink sky, a flock of black crows darted in front of a distant Taj Mahal, providing a teaser of what Agra would bestow come morning.

The hotel's pool was next to useless: too cold in winter and, with temperatures reaching fifty degrees Centigrade in May, no respite in summer. But it was still refreshing to sit by.

'Tell us again why you guys get the best room?' I asked Stew and Reece as we sat down to further dent Brendon's credit card. Both had gloated about their deluxe room with added amenities.

'Why shouldn't we?' asked Reece, scouring the menu.

'Because you guys aren't paying for the trip,' said Brendon.

'The room is under my name,' said Stew, shrugging. 'There's not a lot we can do about it.'

Many young girls watched us play, but not one was allowed to join in.

'And I'm John's second-cousin,' said Reece, relieved he had found a half-adequate answer.

'This isn't a holiday for us,' said Brendon.

'You'll make your money back,' said Reece.

'Not the way you're eating.'

'Speaking of which,' Reece continued, fascinated by a menu the size of a newspaper, 'do you think we should get an entrée as well as dessert?'

'I think I'll need another Kingfisher to make my mind up,' said Stew.

The Taj Mahal and the Fort are the main reasons for visiting Agra. The former, one of the eight wonders of the world, forbids you from entering with food, tobacco, matches, mobile phones or camera tripods. Given the icy temperature at 6.30 am, we were thankful not to be strip-searched — though they did give Stew a good going-over.

'Very fine man!' a nimble-fingered security said, as he felt up the farmer standing on a state-of-the-art wooden crate by the main entrance. The rest of the Black Craps deflated when no such comment came their way.

'Very fine man!' we mocked Stew, once through security. But he knew we were jealous.

The cost to visit one of the finest buildings on earth is seven hundred and fifty rupees for foreigners (about twenty-eight New Zealand dollars) and twenty rupees for locals. I have no problem with this, some would say corrupt, system, and would urge tourist spots at home to do the same. After all, why should a local take his estranged aunt to such a spot for the umpteenth time and pay the same as someone seeing it for the first? The price of the visit, however, soon became irrelevant when we stood like ants at the base of the world's most famous piece of marble.

A monument of love that took twenty thousand workers twenty years to build, the Taj Mahal will make you feel you have achieved absolutely nothing in life!

To stand in front of the Taj Mahal is to feel utterly useless. Something so perfect makes you wonder why we bother. The words 'It just isn't possible' repeat in your floored mind. There are no blemishes, no mistakes, no shortcuts; it's a crime to take a picture and leave. It's a giant, a lion, a cliche, the view and colour changing as each minute passes. It shuts you up. It blinds you. Due to its overwhelming presence, it's easy to ignore the spotless gardens and surrounding mosques, works of mastery in themselves.

'Pretty cool, huh?' said Reece, watching three jaws drop.

'Whooah,' said Brendon.

'Oh my God,' I added.

'Fuck me,' said Stew.

'The Taj Mahal was built as a monument of love by Shah Jahan for his favourite

wife, Mumtaz, who died giving birth to their fourteenth child,' said Reece, kicking into tour guide-speak. 'It took twenty thousand workers twenty years to build. This came at a cost, however, sending the Mughal empire broke. Shah Jahan's son Aurangzeb then killed all his brothers, claimed the throne and imprisoned his father for the rest of his life.'

'Uh-huh,' I said, gaping and gawking.

'Part of the Taj's beauty and mystery is its varied past,' Reece continued. 'Among the stories about its construction is one that claims Shah Jahan had the eyes of one architect gouged out so he could not design another building of its equal.'

'Really?' asked Brendon, more interested in getting a shot no one else had.

'According to the most commonly accepted theory,' added Reece, 'the Taj Mahal was constructed using materials from all over India and Asia. Over a thousand elephants were used to transport building materials during the construction. The white marble was brought from Rajasthan, the jasper from

Punjab and the jade and crystal from China. In all, twenty-eight types of precious and semi-precious stones were inlaid into the white marble. And the total cost of construction was about forty million rupees, at a time when one gram of gold was sold for about 1.3 rupees.'

'Blanket Boy?' said Stew.

'What?'

'Can you just shut up while we look at the building?'

'Charming,' said Reece, miffed. 'Normally when I take tour groups, clients are appreciative and polite. They don't abuse me, they don't make me fill out bloody scorebooks, and they definitely don't wear half-pants.'

'You love us, deep down,' I said.

'Get fucked.'

'You do,' I said.

'No!' He tried not to laugh. 'I don't.'

'You'll miss us when this is all over.'

'Like hell,' he scoffed. 'I'll finally get a good night's sleep.'

'You'll have to pay for your own meals,' said Brendon.

'Okay,' Reece conceded. 'I will miss that.'

If it is true that this most beautiful of monuments was a love letter from Shah Jahan to his wife, it makes a bunch of flowers when in the dog box look pathetically sad. Still, I had to wonder why no one had bombed his creation or at least vandalised it in three hundred and fifty years.

'Can I answer that?' asked Reece.

'Make it funny,' I replied.

'During World War II,' he said, ignoring my comment, 'the Taj was covered in scaffolding and sacking cloth to hide it from bombing raids. The most recent threat is environmental pollution, such as acid rain, which discolours its white marble. The government stepped in fourteen years ago and banned new industrial developments in Agra. Now only non-polluting vehicles are allowed in the immediate vicinity of the Taj Mahal.'

'Where do you store all this shit?' I asked admiringly.

'Yeah,' said Brendon. 'How the hell do you remember it all?'

Reece shrugged, folding his arms under his blanket. 'Drank my own piss for six months?'

Much like the banks of the Ganges, the Taj Mahal is without sound. The shock of silence, coupled with witnessing a man-made piece of magic, is an ethereal experience. Once you reach the steps of the inner compound, your shoes must be covered with white cloths, a piece of elastic around each ankle to stop them from coming off. It was here, as we stood on the marble platform, eyes agape

There is no bad view of the Taj Mahal. You could also add that it's impossible to take a bad photo, but that might offend Brendon . . .

at the Taj's slender white minarets, that I had one of the most significant thoughts of my life.

'Reece,' I said.

'What?'

'We have to have a game here.'

He ignored me. He was busy going weak at the knees, admiring shots Brendon had taken of the Taj.

'Blanket Boy, did you hear me?'

'Yes. You want to have a game here. Fine. What sort of game?'

'Cricket, you idiot.'

'You're having a laugh. There's more security here than at Heathrow.'

'We need to have a game in front of the Taj.'

'Impossible.'

'Hey, there's a river over there,' said Stew, pointing to a stretch of water which accompanied one of the most protected pieces of real estate on earth.

'I suppose we could always play with a view of the Taj,' Brendon said.

'We need to get to that river,' said Stew, adjusting his backpack.

'All right,' said Reece. 'Our driver should know how to get to the river.'

Our driver had no idea of how to get to the river.

e-entering the streets of Agra was like a kick in the balls, the tranquility of the Taj fading faster than the auto-rickshaws we were risking our lives on. When we reached our hotel, we found our driver having a nap. Full of bravado, we asked him to take us to the river with a view of the Taj.

'And then we go to carpet shop?' he asked, wiping sleep from his eyes.

'They're persistent,' said Brendon. 'I'll give them that.'

The more our driver got lost, the more he pretended he wasn't. Then I spotted a beer fridge-sized gap in a corrugated-iron fence. Inside, four kids were playing cricket on a derelict piece of land flanked by, you guessed it, steep brick walls. The batsman had a handkerchief over his face, a necessity on a pitch which resembled Baghdad during a ceasefire. Interest quickly grew: four players became five, then became half of Agra. As usual, Reece bore the brunt, attempting to write names down while Stew and I queried the local rules.

'Over mid-wicket fence is out!' said a boy with the pose of a Bollywood star.

'That's the only rule?' asked Stew.

'Don't let the dog get the ball.'

As we were about to discover, playing cricket in an Agra amphitheatre had its downside. In a typical situation, the surrounding walls would be the perfect solution to errant boundaries. For us, however, it meant that the only way out was via the hole in the fence through which we'd entered. Not that we'd be allowed to do that in a hurry, for our opponents were as zealous as any we had encountered. Reece, in particular, who had suddenly come down with a severe case of Brendonitis, found the cauldron intensely claustrophobic. He soldiered on, and the game began as soon as he told the growing crowd to shut the hell up and start bowling. And to think he used to love India.

Unsurprisingly, a brick was used instead of a shoe to indicate offside wides. The other difference between this and the earlier grounds we had played on was that if you

Dragging the Black Craps into a deserted empty courtyard seemed a good idea at the time. Sadly, the experience brought out the worst in Reece, and eventually all of us.

failed to hit the ball on the full, the petanque court-like surface made it die on the
spot. (Which was a blessing if you were prone to getting bowled.) We batted first
— our opening batsmen both bowled, disproving my theory.

Our other main inconvenience was the scraggy mutt in a singlet who stole the
ball at every available opportunity. Clearly, this was the bugger we'd been warned
about.

'Get him!' everyone yelled. 'Shut the gate!'

When Vicky was retrieved, she was covered in thick, warm saliva, making our
decision to bat a very good one.

Obviously word had got out that the Black Craps were in town. Almost
immediately, we were surrounded by old men, school kids in uniform and
toddlers with candlesticks of snot hanging from their noses. It was bloody
wonderful to see people celebrate cricket to such a degree.

Reece, of course, felt differently. Being choked by dust and surrounded by
scrambling teenagers who squawked 'Shut the gate!' and 'Get him!' as the mutt in
the singlet took Vicky for another run appeared to tip our beloved Jedi Knight over
the edge. 'I feel locked in,' he groaned. 'Please, can we just get out of here?'

For once I believed him. He looked ill, a dead man with a scorebook. The gentlemanly thing to do would have been to offer a supporting hand, or at least a box of stoppers. But as Brendon had sucked the cupboard dry, my only option was to do to Reece what he had done to me.

'Harden up, Blanket Boy,' I said, trying my best to defend a ball on middle brick. 'Just pucker your butt cheeks for a while, then we'll get some lunch.'

'Oh God, lunch,' he groaned, clutching his abdomen.

'You can't eat?' Brendon asked.

'I think I'm going to be sick.'

'You might need some bike clips to keep the shit in!' I finished.

No response. Not good. Get the game over with.

I managed to connect with the last ball of our innings, remembering too late that my six 'over the mid-wicket fence' would actually be my wicket.

'That's okay,' said the keeper. 'You have six.'

Defending a total of twenty-four, India started slowly, eventually needing three runs from the final ball to secure victory. Earlier in that concluding over, four Indian members of the Black Craps argued incessantly over who should deliver the crucial six remaining balls. They bickered and squabbled and fought. Punches were nearly thrown. Earlier in the trip, this behaviour made us laugh; now it was infuriating.

The pleasure and the pain. I find the boundary and the keeper can't believe it. Patel Nagar, Agra.

'I really think I'm going to vomit,' said Reece.

At long last, Irfan bowled the last ball to Sarwal, who hit it high, wide and handsome over the long-on fence. It sailed out into a multitude of cows, stalls and auto-rickshaws. Cue massive jubilation. India had won!

'Okay,' said Reece, tucking the scorebook under his blanket. 'Run for it!'

Four Pied Pipers sprinted down one of Agra's main roads, a hundred kids following close behind. Upon reaching the Goldfish Bowl I realised that, in the mad bid to get away, I had left our bat behind. I started back toward the ground, but was quickly chaperoned in another direction by the Man of the Match, Sarwal, who was yelling at me, inches from my face. 'Your bat! Your bat is running!' He moved his arms about, like those of a jogger, in case I didn't comprehend.

'It's stolen?'

'Yes, sir, it is running!'

The hundred kids hustled me back down the main street. They frantically pointed to nearby houses, but it was no use. It was five minutes since the conclusion of the game; the bat thief would be well gone.

I made for the van, accepting my stupidity. Then, just as the Goldfish Bowl's

PATEL NAGAR, AGRA

BLACK CRAPS

Dhanu (18) bowled Nadim **5**

Jhaked (16) bowled Irfan **0**

Ronu (18) don't know how out **4**

Kadir (13) caught Sarwal **1**

Justin not out **7**

Chan not out **1**

Extras **6**

TOTAL 24

BOWLING

Ibrahim 0-3, Sarwal 0-6, Nadim 1-4,
  Irfan 1-9

INDIA

Ibrahim (20) caught Dhanu **13**

Sarwal (28) not out (two towering
  sixes!) **13**

Nadim (15) bowled **0**

Extras **3**

TOTAL 29

BOWLING

Dhanu 1-12, Ronu 0-5, Justin 0-2,
  Chan 0-7

INDIA WINS
AND TAKES THE SERIES LEAD 4–3.

motor revved, twenty stoic young detectives appeared out of nowhere, sprinting down the middle of the road. They held our bat in the air, as if it were the Cricket World Cup. 'Your bat!' they screamed. 'Your bat!'

Another game, another loss. This time, however, we had a thief to contend with. Patel Nagar, Agra.

Sarwal, the happiest guy with no teeth I've ever met, did the honours, handing the piece of willow to Stew through the back window, tipping his Auckland Aces cap as he did. The kids chased us as we fled, whacking the van's bumper and windows. From the inside, it felt as though we were being pelted by horizontal hailstones.

Safely in our cocoon, Reece resumed his near-death appearance.

'I'm really sorry about that, fellas,' I puffed.

'You will be,' said Reece.

'Honestly,' I pleaded, 'there were only four kids when I first spotted them. I thought it was going to be a quick, relaxing game.'

'You'll pay for this,' he added, wiping his brow and throwing the scorebook onto the back seat.

'And we fucking lost,' said Stew.

TWELVE

Previous page: The outfield needs work, but what a view. The first game of our tour to involve match-fixing. Kachpura Village, Agra.

A MATCH WITH RAJA FEDERER

Our driver eventually found the river, but not before going grey. We thanked him as he parked the Goldfish Bowl by archaic carts selling chewing gum, stale chips and Thums Up cola, all of which were frying in the midday sun. The river itself was a five-hundred-metre walk along a sandy path surrounded by shacks and dense foliage. A young boy named Hasin joined us, along with his younger sister and brother. Polite and upbeat, together they directed us to a view of the Taj which had Brendon almost literally wetting his pants.

'Oh yes!' he said, unloading camera paraphernalia. 'This is great!'

'I think he likes it,' said Reece.

And so did the rest of us, the ridiculous drive through Agra's tangled mess worth every minute. The Taj from this angle was a dreamy silhouette, the mist in the foreground only adding to its allure. The Yamuna River — which provided its reflection — however, didn't hold quite the same draw. One of the most polluted rivers in the world, with fifty-seven million people depending on its waters, the Yamuna leaves Delhi as a sewer, burdened with the city's biological and chemical wastes. Downstream, where we stood, was Agra's main municipal drinking water source. The treatment facilities are no match for the poisons. As a result, those living in Delhi and Agra consume unknown amounts of toxic pesticide residues each time they drink water. A picture-postcard view it might have been, but the liquid rubbish dump before us denied our favoured match spot a place on any tourist map.

The twelve-year-old with the camel was Brijesh. His perfect English and Bollywood smile meant that our cheery helper, Hasin, was momentarily shoved to one side. He appeared to accept his fate as if it were a regular occurrence, handing the reins to the boy with the camel — and the confidence.

'This is Raja, my camel,' Brijesh boasted. 'You want picture?'

'Roger?' I asked.

'Yes, Raja.'

'As in Raja Moore?' added Stew.

'Or Raja Federer?' I said.

'How about Raja Rabbit?' said Brendon.

We thought we were hilarious, but Brijesh had work to do. His mannerisms — quick wit, shifty smile, carefully chosen language — resembled Paul Newman's in *The Hustler*. Everything was a deal. Everything was for sale.

'You want to play cricket?' he asked upon seeing our bat.

'Sure,' Stew said, looking around. 'But we need more players.'

Quick as a wink, Brijesh grabbed the bat and leaned on it like Greg Chappell on a hundred and fifty. 'We keep the bat here,' he said. 'You come back at 3 pm.'

'Why 3 pm?' I asked.

'That's when kids finish school.'

'How come you're not at school?' Brendon asked.

'I don't need to go to school.'

It was a bribe and it worked. But Brijesh wasn't quite finished. 'If India wins later,' he said as we were leaving, 'we keep your bat.'

'And what if New Zealand wins?' I asked.

'If New Zealand wins,' he answered slowly, thoughts whirring freely in his uncomplicated business head, 'we serve you tea.'

We fell for that one too, later appreciating what a master plan it really was. After all, if we didn't turn up, Brijesh would get a free bat. If we did turn up, he'd get a game of cricket. The only issue for us was one of traffic, Agra's choked arterials making Kolkata and Delhi look positively sedate, even orderly. But we had no choice. We had to get back by 3 pm to claim our bat and beat India in front of the Taj Mahal.

Now someone just had to tell our driver.

long with contracting yet another version of Delhi Belly, Brendon was suffering from stiff joints and achy muscles from all that lugging of camera gear. When he told us he was shouting himself a massage for 'professional reasons', we had no choice but to believe him. While he did this and Reece and Stew watched TV in

their room, I accidentally gatecrashed a yoga session. In a room containing three mats and an ego, a calm (too calm, if you ask me) former army sergeant spoke slowly and surely, with the conviction of a BBC children's presenter. The only other victim, a middle-aged woman from Bristol, warmed up while I admired our instructor's perfect feet, which matched his equally wrinkle-free white pyjamas.

I like yoga, having tried it a few times when my first daughter was a baby. I couldn't go for runs while she slept, so instead risked serious injury on a daily basis following instructions from the *Get Your Body Back* DVD. (Yes, it is designed for women trying to lose weight after giving birth, but I did have the curtains closed.) Imagine my horror, then, when having completed what I thought was a near-perfect Warrior, Camel and Dog pose, our Indian instructor dissected our techniques.

'You very good!' he said to the Brit.

He then briefly focused on me. Memories from school came flooding back. 'You,' he scoffed, 'not so good.'

'All right, mate,' I managed. 'Don't rub it in.'

But I was speaking too fast, plus he had little interest in someone with the flexibility of a curtain rod. More worrying for me, however, was whether I'd be paying for this session or, as I hoped, it was a freebie with the room. This concern did not aid relaxation or well-being.

'Every day, we run, run, run!' our instructor continued, achieving a position I thought only possible for women half his age. 'And why? Let us look no further than household pets. Dogs: they pant, pant, pant!'

He emulated a dog puffing. I suppressed a laugh.

'Dogs live for thirteen years at the most!' he exclaimed. 'Ha! Now, look at the tortoise: a s-l-o-w animal that takes d-e-e-p breaths, lives to a hundred and fifty.'

I wanted to say that genetic make-up probably contributes more to an animal's longevity than the speed at which it gets around, but who was I to argue? Next, he had us performing an extremely awkward Butterfly pose, but not before embarrassing me again in front of my only classmate.

'You,' he said to her, 'very good.'

He hovered over my left shoulder. I knew what was coming. 'You, not so good.'

Never trust a man who doesn't sweat or swear.

Despite my being ridiculed, my fix was a damn sight cheaper than Brendon's. 'Didn't you have to pay for yours?' he asked, looking half-asleep after a rigorous rubdown.

'I don't think so,' I replied. 'Anyway, if I do, it'll be on your credit card.'

'Speaking of which,' said Stew, helping himself to more bhuja, 'let's get another beer before lunch.'

'Be rude not to,' I said.

My phone beeped.

FROM JOHN BOUGEN:
STILL STUCK IN VIENNA, PLANE
DELAYED. HOW'S BRENDON'S ARSE?

Rush hour Agra-style. We needed to get to a 3 pm game.

It was 2 pm. Knowing the river was at least an hour's drive away, we hit the road. There was no question that we wanted to play; we just continued to struggle with Agra's wayward herds of buffalo, auto-rickshaws driven like go-carts, and smoke-spluttering motorised hairdryers doing their best to demolish every available wing-mirror by squeezing through outrageously narrow gaps. Agra traffic was a sitcom but really, what did we have to complain about? The city's drivers, each battling for pole position, were actually doing something useful. We were just making sure we didn't lose our cricket bat.

By 3 pm we had reached the river and the boys were waiting with our bat, secretly hoping, I'm sure, that we weren't going to turn up. Once more, word of our arrival had got out: an ever-increasing crowd, tourists included, stood on the Yamuna's adjacent sand dunes.

Brijesh walked over with Raja and looked us right in the eye. 'Right,' he said. 'You made it. Let us start.'

His manner was admirable, if a little irritating. He seemed destined for stardom, not the street — the words 'mafia' and 'millionaire' were not far from one's mind when watching him in action. He also seemed smart enough to know

he had to make his own luck. 'I've been in many books and TV shows on India,' he said, striking a pose.

Then, like a wave of nausea, came the part Blanket Boy despised. Thankfully, an agreeable lunch had cheered him up somewhat but I'm sure that, given the choice, he would have hurled the scorebook, which hung from his blanket like a ball and chain, into the Yamuna at the first opportunity. When at last he scribbled down some sort of disorder, we started a game in front of a monument which deserved better.

'Okay,' said Reece, losing his patience. 'New Zealand bat first. Let's go!'

'Six a side, six overs each,' said Stew, taking guard.

I took my place as umpire at the bowler's end, while Brijesh expertly guided Raja the camel to the deep fine-leg boundary before marking out his run-up.

One of the advantages of playing your home ground is the prerogative to cheat. It is your god-given right. One small requirement, however, is letting your opposition know of any homespun rules in advance. In this case, our first mistake was to bat first, unaware of the local 'free-hit' rule.

Things were about to get heated. But not before Stew, clearly conserving energy for the big games, butchered Vicky in front of an expectant, appreciative crowd.

Still irate at his golden duck in Darjeeling, he dispatched almost every delivery over cow's corner for six, his lunch diet of Kingfishers and curry a well-kept — if quick single-preventing — secret. All up, he smashed five sixes, some of which had frantic searchers scouring the sand dunes for the offending shot. Reece could barely keep up with his room-mate's antics, hurriedly scrawling down what resembled an international phone number: 4, 1, 1, 1, 1, 6, 6, 6, 6, 6, 1.

When Vicky rolled into the river due to misdirected square cuts, we stood back and let our opposition retrieve her, knowing that people were being burned downstream. It was also a good time to catch up on the real reason people visit Agra. In the fading light, the Taj continued to dazzle. It was beyond grand, the spectacle addictive.

Did these kids realise how special this place was? Hardly. To them, it was just a cricket ground with an annoying water trap at deep cover.

'Wait!' I said, upon seeing Brijesh begin a second over. 'One over each, that was the rule.'

'No,' said Brijesh defiantly. 'Two overs maximum.'

I looked to Stew, who mouthed 'Whatever' and belted the next ball to Rajasthan.

'That's over,' I said at the conclusion of Brijesh's effort, tossing Vicky to a fielder with 'Murder' written on his shirt.

'Hang on,' yelled Reece. 'I've only got six balls!'

'Yeah,' I replied. 'That's what's you call an over.'

'But I thought there was a no-ball.'

'I thought you had the hang of this,' said Brendon.

'So who's bowling now?'

'Sunil the murderer,' I replied.

Reece looked down at his scorebook.

> Reece, about to have a mental breakdown for the eighth time on the trip. India is not happy with proceedings, particularly the boy with 'Murder' written on his shirt.

'But I have Sunil down for New Zealand, not India.'

'He changed teams,' said Brijesh. 'He is now India.'

While such nonsense occurred, there were dozens of perfectly capable younger boys loitering. They would have given anything to play, but were bulldozed by louder voices and pushier attitudes. Stew, having retired on thirty-eight, provided the backbone for the Black Craps, and we were confident at the innings break. As we approached Reece to tell him of our bowling order, a man with terrible eyes stood over his shoulder. Blanket Boy was concentrating on the job at hand so didn't immediately see what we did: eyes with no pupils, whites only, a hint of smoky yellow. They were the eyes of a fish after it has been steamed. The beggar held his hand out, saying, 'I'm blind.'

Reece, who had now caught a glimpse but was still focused on those damn no-balls, replied, 'I can see!'

'No need to rub it in,' said Stew.

efending the highest score of our tour, we were complacently delirious. Even more so when Brijesh was caught by Meenu having scored just one run. This was to be our only success. Once Brijesh took over as umpire, the good days were over.

'No-ball,' he said to my next delivery. 'And free hit.'

'Yes!' said the batsman at the striker's end, raising his bat baseball-style.

'Free hit! Free hit!' yelled an ecstatic India.

'What do you mean, "free hit"?' Stew asked.

'You bowled a no-ball. Free hit after,' said Sunil the murderer.

'You never told us that when we were batting,' I said.

The Indians shrugged their shoulders. I secretly admired them. Don't ask, don't get. Brijesh now took it upon himself to take cheating to an epic level, calling us for no-balls even when we hadn't overstepped. This, of course, meant his batsmen could have an almighty swing at the next delivery without fear of losing their wicket. Brijesh was the kid who had all the gear but none of the talent. Hell-bent on winning, and in no hurry to make friends, his failure with the bat only exacerbated the situation.

One thing was for sure: dirty tactics meant that the Black Craps now had a real scrap on their hands. Stew and I decided that the only solution was to stand by Brijesh as our bowlers ran up to the crease. Unrepentant, he continued to no-ball every second ball.

'Free hit!' he yelled to his batsman.

Naturally, with pressure averted, the next ball joined the locals sitting on the sand dunes. We were dealing with a serial cheat, but could do nothing. Backyard cricketers can't complain to the BCCI (Board of Control for Cricket in India). We could only attempt to stem the flow. As for taking wickets, we couldn't buy one, despite having extra fielders in the form of goats, buffalo and Roger the camel.

Amid the carnage, however, one player who didn't cheat or go out was our killer, Sunil. He had obviously taken a leaf out of Stew's book, eventually hitting the winning runs with ease and, in doing so, ensuring our second loss of the day.

'Mind you,' I said as we shook hands with our opponents, 'I bet international cricketers don't get up at dawn to look at the city's highlights on match day.'

'Poor excuse, Justin,' said Brendon.

And he was right, but we needed some way to cover up our pitiful showing. One player, you may have guessed, who wasn't going to go quietly was Raja's owner. Incredibly, despite his unique umpiring, Brijesh continued to push for glory. 'I win! I win!' he jumped up and down. 'I am Man of the Match!'

'Don't think so, mate,' I said. 'Sunil top-scored.'

'I win!' repeated Brijesh.

Sunil accepted his prize with a sheepish grin.

'New Zealand is bad,' Brijesh said, giving us the thumbs-down. 'I win!'

'Your team won,' said Stew.

'No,' said Brijesh. 'I win!'

Seeing the bat resting on the stumps, he quickly grabbed it, the second time today such an attempted abduction had occurred. 'Captain keeps the bat!'

Two boys walked us back to the Goldfish Bowl. One was Sunil, the Man of the Match; the other was Hasin, our helper from earlier in the day. We decided to give him a cap, too. He was such a cool kid, with

Two things India has in abundance: home-made balls and keen cricketers.

a gentle nature and tough life. His mother had 'expired', he had told us, so he had to look after his sister and five younger brothers.

It was little surprise to discover that Tendulkar and Ponting were both boys' favourite players. Of more interest were their chosen career goals. 'I want to be an engineer,' said Hasin.

'And what about you, Sunil?' Reece asked the bloke with 'Murder' on his shirt. The answer came quickly: 'I want to be a doctor.'

Once again, the most unlikely of us to own moisturising gel passed it around the van as if it was gold. Until now, Stew had cleansed his farm-beaten hands after each match without us noticing but now we'd discovered his secret.

'Stops you getting sick,' he said.

'Too late,' said Brendon.

'Second that,' added Reece.

Each Black Crap savoured the moment, rubbing his hands together and

Raja the camel patrols third slip . . . before heading off for drinks.

smelling the result. It's the little things.

'Well,' I said, looking at the scorebook from the latest ill-fated offering, 'we're officially up shit creek. Five-three down, with only Jaipur and Mumbai to go.'

'It would help if they didn't cheat,' said Stew.

'Maybe we need to start cheating.'

'We're playing kids,' said Brendon.

'We're losing to kids.'

Agra rolled by, its workers and occupants staring at four grown men handing around moisturiser. It would be another hour before we reached the hotel. In the meantime, our vehicular refuge was a good way to catch up on normality. Stew spoke to his family on his mobile while I viewed a text from mine saying they were off to sing Christmas carols at the Auckland Domain. Earlier in the day, Brendon had spoken to — and watched — his one-year-old daughter thousands of miles away via Skype.

'I don't know what you guys are worried about,' said Reece. 'I mean, aren't these games just a bunch of friendlies with kids?'

The ensuing silence, coupled with stern looks, said it all.

JAMUNA BRIDGE, KACHPURA VILLAGE, AGRA

BLACK CRAPS

Stew retired!	38
Hasin caught Sunil	0
Chota Patan caught Brijesh	2
Meenu not out	9
Justin not out	2
Extras	7
TOTAL.	**58**

BOWLING

Brijesh 1-17 (two overs), Parveen
0-4 (one over), Sahab Singh 0-9
(one over), Sunil 1-28 (two overs)

INDIA

Brijesh caught Meenu	1
Parveen bowled Justin	0
Sahab Singh run out (Stew)	0
Sunil not out	36
Raj Kumar caught Justin	5
Anand not out.	4
Extras	15
TOTAL.	**61**

BOWLING

Stew 1-8, Justin 2-17 (two overs),
Hasin 0-8, Meenu 1-24 (two overs)

INDIA WINS AND TAKES 5–3 LEAD.

It feels awful even in front of
the Taj. Parveen loses his middle
stump. Kachpura Village, Agra.

he next trip was back to Delhi by train. Waiting in the hotel's lobby for our driver, we had two choices: get our palms read or read a newspaper. As the fortune-teller hadn't enlightened a single customer since we had arrived, we opted for real life. Which wasn't such a sound choice, going by Reece's look of horror upon seeing the cover of the *Hindustan Times*.

FATAL ATTACK
A visitor lies dead outside an enclosure for Royal Bengal tigers after he was attacked by two tigers at the zoo in Guwahati on Wednesday. The visitor was trying to take a picture of the two tigers from up close when they caught him and ripped off his left hand, triggering a fatal haemorrhage.

The article, accompanied by one of the most gruesome pictures I've ever seen, took up a quarter of the front page. It showed a man lying on his back outside the tiger enclosure, looking as though he had been killed in a bomb blast. There was no evidence of a left arm. His white shirt was claret-red, his face sprayed by blood which had obviously shot out from the hole in his torso. Unfathomably, somebody had taken that photo before calling for help. And the tiger was still in shot at the top of the frame.

With another hour to fill before departure, I found an internet cafe, one of possibly millions in this computer giant of a land. There I found that Anna had made the news back in New Zealand. *The New Zealand Herald* had an article about the 'fearless New Zealander who always wanted to do things the average person wouldn't think of doing'. I looked at the screen for a long time. By now John would nearly be in Egypt, having to deal with the unbearable. I remembered back to when he and Anna used to have us around for dinner. Anna, a wonderful cook, would whip up fantastic dishes while her husband and I dreamed crazy dreams. She was great, too, with our daughter, giving her a floppy yellow cow which quickly became her favourite toy.

Life sucks sometimes.

he 2001 Shatabdi Express to New Delhi should take two and a half hours, so we would hit the capital again around 2300 hours. However, since Indian Railways is one of the busiest and largest networks in the world, with well over one and a half million employees, we knew this was optimistic. While we waited, beggars raided the platform, including a break-dancing toddler whose moves convinced Reece to treat him to a packet of biscuits. In his diary, Stew put it well: 'Everywhere we've been we've found kids who deserve better in their lives.'

Once on the carriage, life returned to normal. That is, Reece ate soup with his

fingers while the rest of India used knives and forks. The less adventurous Black Craps didn't eat the main, but devoured the vanilla ice cream.

'Hello, dear, I'm standing opposite the most magnificent building ever made! No, we're not going through it, we're playing cricket with a bunch of cheats by a polluted river!'

When the 2001 Shatabdi Express stopped in the middle of the boonies for over an hour, we wondered whether the number on the train was the last time she'd had a proper check-up. The only way to tolerate such a delay was for Stew and me to sing 'Hello Delhi'. Despite arriving at 1 am, we found our dour mood soon fading when we discovered that we were about to spend the night in a palace. But not before Stew got into a fight.

THIRTEEN

Previous page: Reece negotiates wides and no-balls from his beloved scorebook. Dry lake bed opposite Amber Fort, Jaipur.

SNAKE-CHARMERS IN THE PINK CITY

Here's how it happened. Four deadbeat travellers get off a train at Delhi. Despite their acclimatisation to India, they are still shocked at the number of beggars sleeping inside the train station. They are desperate to find a bed for the night, but upon reaching the exit they see the farmer being harassed by a stranger. The rest keep walking. Suddenly, the stranger tries to take the farmer's backpack. The farmer yells, 'Hey, get out of it.' The stranger mutters something but persists with the aim of taking the farmer's bag, this time yanking it so hard it falls from the farmer's shoulder. The farmer, now irate and quickly losing patience, retrieves his bag and yells 'Fuck off' before giving the thief a short, sharp thwack on the arm. The thief, looking offended, retreats and cowers, looking to the rest of the group for guidance. But they are too busy crying with laughter. They eventually inform the farmer that the man trying to take his bag is their driver.

Delhi. Again. No one took the travel for granted; it's just that seeing the same city three times — and one we hadn't fallen in love with — was like being held back a year at school. Any hint of disappointment, however, quickly vanished once we reached the hotel John had secretly booked as a treat. The Taj Palace was exactly that, a hotel with a foyer the size of a village and polished floors that sparkled like a lake. Most of the people who walked through its front doors wore what looked like thousands of dollars worth of jewellery. Stew took multiple photos of its incredible paintings for his art-crazy wife, Jess. Porters, cleaners and maitre d's smiled at every corner, looking like an army waiting for its general.

Such fuss is difficult for your average backpacker to comprehend, and reminded me of when I spoke to New Zealand cricketer Scott Styris about the treatment he received in India's five-star hotels. When he first visited the subcontinent, he couldn't believe players like Ganguly and Dravid clicking their fingers and an apologetic waitress arriving seconds later with toast. Alas, it seems that humans are versatile beings, and he was able to imitate his opponents' behaviour days later. But the Indians were in for a rude shock when they toured New Zealand. Styris told me of the time they sat down to breakfast at a hotel with far fewer amenities than Indian cricket gods were used to. When the said players clicked their fingers and demanded 'More toast!' they received a slightly less obliging reaction.

'Yeah,' said the bubblegum-chewing waitress. 'You know where it is.'

Being treated to five-star-plus didn't stop Brendon and me from going for the jugular, making Stew and Reece hold true on a verbal contract they had made on the train. The agreement was to let the idiots paying for their part of the trip take the room booked under the name of Bougen at the next stop. This suited Reece and Stew just fine, especially with the news given to us by the woman at reception. 'I'm very sorry, gentlemen,' she smiled. 'We don't seem to have your room. Would you like an upgrade?'

The upgrade meant the Club Taj on the seventh floor. With a business centre, conference facilities and complimentary deluxe continental breakfast, it covered all possible requirements for three hobos and a man in a blanket. As we shuffled towards bed past spotless staff dressed in morning suits, they all uttered polite greetings but clearly wondered how we'd made it past security.

Our two rooms were exactly the same, but only an idiot would complain. Along with the obligatory chocolates and fresh guava juice was a, wait for it, pillow menu:

Breath easy pillow
Cotton pillow
Dream pillow
Feather down pillow
Neck comforting pillow
Sound sleep pillow
Polly fill pillow

Brendon and I were both asleep before hitting our allocated pillows, so there wasn't much point in hassling reception for a replacement. The next morning, after one of those undisturbed slumbers that only hours on the road can bring, we woke to find three newspapers at our door. We had overslept and breakfast was waiting.

Stew and Blanket Boy were waiting for us in the dining room on our floor. The Executive Breakfast was no more than fifty steps away. Waitresses in black miniskirts served us fresh coffee. Businessmen sat talking matters of state while we ordered more toast. This was all very different from what we knew lay on the street seven floors below. The only blot on an otherwise pristine landscape smelt of chlorine and hung from Reece's shoulders.

'For the love of God,' said Stew, holding his nose, 'it's breakfast. Take that bloody blanket off.'

'Why?' asked an offended Reece.

'All I can smell is formaldehyde.'

'I had it washed.'

'You smell like a chemical plant,' I said.

'Rubbish,' Reece said, putting old faithful on the back of his chair.

'Not there,' Stew said. 'Put it away properly. It stinks to high heaven.'

Reece opened a door to the antique cupboard behind our table and put his cape next to some sparkling, meticulously ordered cutlery.

If there was a God, I thought, he would forget he had put it there.

he time after breakfast was spent avoiding the inevitable: planning two days in Delhi before flying to Jaipur. There was India Gate, a war memorial commemorating the members of the Indian Army who lost their lives fighting in World War I and the Afghan Wars. And a visit to New Delhi's wonderfully clean and well-organised parliamentary sector. But nothing could beat a phone call I received while on the toilet at day's end.

Earlier, Brendon and I, utterly knackered from being tourists for the day, had watched the entire bath scene from *Pretty Woman* before one of us had the energy to reach for the remote. And then came the phone call that made me want to hang up my backpacking boots forever.

'Good afternoon,' I said, my voice echoing around the bathroom.

'Hello, Mr Bougen?'

It was a lot easier to say yes than explain the real situation. 'This is him,' I said.

'I'm Kavita Aneja,' said the sweet-sounding voice on the end of the line. 'Guest Relations Manager of the Taj Palace.'

'Hello, Kavita. What's up?'

'I was wondering whether you would care to join us for cocktails in Room 105?'

'Cocktails?'

'Yes. We are also having other guests, but would love to see you there.'

'Why, yes,' I said with a plum in my mouth. 'That would be lovely.'

'Excellent,' said Kavita. 'See you at 7 pm.'

I put the phone back on the wall above

In Rajasthan, a good moustache proves the virility of a man. Our doorman in Jaipur had little to worry about in that department.

the toilet roll, washed my hands and found Brendon lying on his bed, channel-surfing. 'Who was that?' he asked, eyes not leaving the screen.

'Kavita,' I replied. 'Put your tails on, we're going to a party.'

I located my 'going out' jandals and had an Aussie shower (splashed on some deodorant). Indeed, because this party was something special, I even sponged the front of my trousers. We made our way to Room 105, replying to half a dozen 'Good evening, sirs' on the way. We felt like frauds. 'Now, no silly stuff,' I said, ringing the doorbell of Room 105.

'Yeah right,' scoffed Stew.

A very attractive woman, spick and span in black and white, stood before four homeless hacks. This was Kavita. The room was like any other in the hotel, the only difference being the free champagne poured by four equally well-dressed men who stood to attention in each corner.

Collectively the Black Craps possessed many handicaps, but bullshitting was not one of them. We could do it anywhere, anytime. In this case, the more right answers we provided — more to the point, the more answers our Guest Relations Manager wanted to hear — the more free booze we were given. And the less we had to spend on dinner. Which was something I made a little too clear when the salmon and caviar came around for the third time: 'Saves us buying food from the restaurant tonight.'

'Sshh!' said Blanket Boy, almost spluttering his bacon-wrapped green beans across the table.

A family from Newcastle soon joined us: mum, dad and two sons. The eldest son had been studying in India, one of the reasons his parents had made the trip. Small talk resumed and then jealousy, Dad clearly wanting to join us the next morning in preference to visiting tourist spots with his family.

'Now,' said Kavita, finding a minuscule gap in a conversation about cricket, champagne and Jackson Pollock-esque toilet adventures, 'if there were a way we could improve the Taj Palace, what would it be?'

She clicked her pen and readied herself for answers, of which there were none. The main problem with the question was the small matter of there being not one thing wrong with the hotel. Another problem was that no answer would bring no more food and no more grog. I poked Reece in the ribs. 'Come on,' I said, with the desperation of a drunk, 'think of something.'

Stew, seeing the end was nigh, sculled the contents of his champagne glass and had a waiter refill it. Brendon ate a sweet-and-sour meatball. Kavita's pen hovered over the clipboard. For the first time in the past hour, we were silent.

We were back in school.

'Ooh,' said Reece, probably a little too enthusiastically, 'I know.'

We looked at him as if he were Jesus. Could this man, without the aid of his putrid safety blanket, pave the way towards an extended good life of caviar and bubbles? Or had we, as expected, been outed as the true con artists we really were?

He spoke at last. 'We only have one reading lamp on the wall above our bed.'

Reece shuffled. Kavita looked up from her notes. At first she looked as if she was going to scold, as if Blanket Boy had just admitted he was going to marry her only sister. Then she squinted, cocked her head, and just stared.

This we took to be very good, or very bad.

'That's true!' Kavita smiled. 'The rooms do only have one lamp.'

Reece sat up. He really was Jesus. And all without the blanket. 'I mean, what if a couple want their own light?'

'Exactly!' Kavita enthused, scribbling every word down.

'More champagne?' asked a white-gloved man with a full bottle.

'Don't mind if I do,' said Reece. 'Our work here is done.'

Twenty-four hours later Delhi's fog once more brought us to our knees. What was supposed to be a forty-five-minute flight to Jaipur was now a conundrum: should we drive six hours north, arriving at midnight, or fly to Rajasthan the following morning if the weather allowed? The worst part of this news was our complacent assumption that the van ride to Agra had been our last on India's roads. The second-worst part was the way Sunil grinned as he told us. The Indian technique of selling bad news with a smile is sweet, but a little disconcerting. An unhappy tourist is a dangerous being; one who thinks he's leaving Delhi, only to discover that his plane hates the place as much as he does, is another beast altogether.

Thankfully the Black Craps were all fans of waking up to a new city. And so it was that we boarded the Goldfish Bowl, battled Delhi's rush hour and headed towards the final piece of the golden triangle. Although it is hard to admit, the only thing able to lift our spirits at 10.47 pm on a dusty, pothole-ridden highway was the Golden Arches. Even Brendon, once again at war with his arse, agreed that the best cure was a spicy McMaharaja burger. We stood at the counter like ten-year-olds at a birthday party. Brendon was Dad, and we were the annoying little shits who wanted two of everything. Apart from signs written in Hindi, and Bollywood songs on the radio, we might as well have been in New York, New Lynn or Newfoundland.

Amid the chaos, India's architecture is detailed and beautiful.

Despite ordering double for everyone, the feed barely touched the sides, each of us scouring paper bags in vain for leftovers. We did, however, make sure we ate in the van to ensure we would reach Jaipur this side of midnight. A text message welcomed us into a new mobile network, then beeped again minutes later.

FROM JOHN BOUGEN:
FINISHED MY BOOK — HAVE YOU?

The failure to finish *Shantaram*, the brick disguised as a book, continued to gnaw away at me every time I repacked it. Here was a story of an escaped Australian convict who became a doctor in the slums of Mumbai, and wrote about it with rare lucidity. Leopold's, the expat bar where he carried out dodgy dealings in the 1980s with similarly dodgy characters, was so well described you wanted to go there right away. But then the author loses the plot, the hero goes to fight a war in Afghanistan, finds the girl of his dreams, sleeps around on her, finds her again, sleeps around on her. At nine hundred pages, it was seven hundred pages too long.

But the first two hundred and twenty were unbeatable.

Upon reaching Jaipur, we were greeted at the hotel by a walking moustache. The doorman was wearing something like sherwani, the long robes which are often still worn by Indian grooms and in times past were the court clothes of Rajput warriors. But we were more intrigued by this man's perfectly trimmed face fuzz. Moustaches prove the virility of a Rajput man, so the longer the better, although various castes and tribes have different ways of growing and tying them. The man before us, however, had little to worry about in that department, possessing chops that would put Thomas Magnum to shame.

We were shown to our rooms. The draw of shut-eye after six hours on the highway was like a magnet. We slept the sleep of kings, but for one minor incident. At 3 am I woke to find Brendon in the single bed next to mine, laughing like a hyena.

'What?' I managed, still trying to work out where I was.

'You don't know?'

He was still sniggering.

'No, what?'

He laughed some more. And couldn't stop. I started to get tetchy. Clearly I had done something I promised wouldn't happen again on the trip. Brendon composed himself, and managed to talk without hooting. 'You sat up, and said, "Hello! Hello! Hello! Hello!"' He said, 'Hello!' as if he was Gollum in *The Lord of the Rings.*

'Crap,' I said.

'You did! How could I make that up?'

'No word of this at breakfast.'

'Oh yeah, okay.'

Breakfast was a nightmare. Three Gollums and a defenceless sleepwalker going at it hammer and tongs. Brendon held court, savouring every detail of my misfortune. I admired everybody's ability to annoy.

'Only sleepwalks once every couple of months.'

'Yeah right.'

'At least he didn't leave his room this time.'

'Hello! Hello! Hello!'

Rebuttal is impossible when you don't know what it was you actually did. The best thing to do was promise that such an occurrence wouldn't happen again before departure. Brendon's response wasn't encouraging: he laughed harder than when he had found me screaming at 3 am.

An obese American woman sat one table over with her teenage daughter. When a waiter, more refined and respectful than she could ever be, placed a can of Pepsi in front of her she barked, 'I said Diet! And where's the ice?'

Sonu was looking good with the bat but sadly had to retire as he had a customer to attend to.

Having disposed of the restaurant's supply of toast, we moved outside to be greeted by the ever-faithful Goldfish Bowl. It was easily our warmest morning yet. We celebrated by leaving sweatshirts behind and exposing knees and shins.

'You're really making no attempt to blend in, are you?' said Reece.

'Not really,' I said.

'It's a beautiful day,' said Brendon.

'You look like labourers and schoolboys,' said Reece. 'Look at Stew, he's not wearing half-pants.'

'I haven't worn them since the start of the trip,' said Stew.

'There's a respectful tourist for you,' said Reece.

'Thank you, Blanket Boy,' nodded the farmer.

I looked at Stew's perfect attire and the smug look on his face. 'Teacher's pet,' I said.

aipur, the capital of Rajasthan, is built from pink stucco (a material made of an aggregate, binder and water), made to resemble sandstone. For this reason, the showcase of Rajasthani architecture is known as the Pink City. It's almost as if its founders scored a summer special on pink paint, started on a Saturday morning and never stopped. The result, however, is far from dull. But why pink? The city was painted that colour in 1853 to welcome the Prince of Wales, pink being the traditional Rajput colour of welcome.

Jaipur is less hectic than other major Indian cities. And it shows in its inhabitants, many of whom just hang out, meet up, or just pass the time. On the hilltops, forts and palaces remind the traveller of a more regal era. Elephants and camels clog roads, creating traffic jams the photographer in the back seat couldn't pass up on. Soon we passed Jal Mahal (literally Water Palace), a pleasure fortress built in 1799. Five storeys high, with its first floors underwater in Mansagar Lake, it was built for royal duck-shooting parties. A giant iceberg of a building that now

lay abandoned, it was a birdwatcher's paradise, but visibly not one immune to leaky building syndrome.

Our plan was to find cricket with a view. Our driver, as usual, had other ideas. 'Elephant ride?' he asked as the van wound its way up the hillside.

'Here we go again,' said Reece. 'No thanks, gee!'

'Jantar Mantar?'

'No thanks.'

'City Palace Museum?'

'No.'

'Jawahar Circle?'

'Nope.'

'Birla Temple?'

'Fuggoff,' said Stew. 'Just find us a spot where we can play cricket, gee.'

omething Jaipur doesn't have, but clearly needs, is a plural for the word 'palace'. They are everywhere. Forts, too, like Nahagarh, which, while a remarkable structure with grand views and individual rooms for each of the king's nine wives, was a terrible venue for a quick ten-over game. That's because the only player we could find was a 'guide' who had attached himself to us like a limpet. The only option was to head back down the hill. Our driver hit the outskirts of town and parked the Goldfish Bowl next to half a dozen tourist jeeps, a renovated palace as a backdrop.

The building was Amber Fort, military headquarters of the Kachhwa dynasty of Jaipur rulers. By the speed at which a teenage snake-charmer joined us, we figured this was a regular tourist spot. He opened a basket more suited to picnics. A cobra woke from a slumber and lethargically projected itself upwards. The boy regularly tapped him. The snake appeared irritated, but performed when the boy played his flute. At the end of his number, the snake-charmer held his hand out, but we were more interested in the possibility of playing cricket on a dry lake bed.

Aitram, the first ever snake-charmer to play cricket for New Zealand.

'Could turn a bit,' said a musing Stew.

'Not exactly a green top,' I replied.

Before we knew it, we had enough Amber Fort jeep drivers for a game. In a genius move, one of which Brijesh the cheat would be proud, the Black Craps secured the services of the snake-charmer.

'Now, let's not do what we did in Agra,' I said, tossing the ball to Stew. 'Remember, these guys have unwritten laws.'

'Any no-ball or wide is a free hit,' he replied.

'No runs for legs byes or byes.'

'Can't be bowled on a full toss.'

'It's a no-ball if it bounces more than once.'

'Are you getting all this, Blanket Boy?' Brendon asked.

'Nope,' said Reece.

'Any full toss is a no-ball,' I continued.

'If you don't tell the umpire what you're bowling, it's a no-ball.'

'Same with change of wicketkeeper.'

'Jesus, you lot,' said Reece. 'I thought cricket was a simple game.'

'Not in India,' said Stew.

The main issue with playing against jeep drivers was keeping them on the field. Understandably, whenever a tourist arrived or they received a radio call from their vehicle, they abandoned the game at pace. Even the umpire was a driver; he leapt away to a waiting customer before the end of the first over. Another, Sonu, did the same thing, retiring on zero. The outfield wasn't much. We spent most of the match dodging camel shit and boulders the size of soccer balls.

Then, with just one over to go in India's innings, Vicky packed a sad. She split in two, obviously tiring of the constant beltings she had received. Thankfully, our drivers had a plan. 'One hundred rupees, sir,' said Rarman, the driver. 'We buy two more balls.'

Reece temporarily stopped scoring and handed over two fifties. Rarman sped off in his jeep, leaving dust, rocks and customers in his wake. Within five minutes, he returned with two cherry-red Vickys.

The jeep drivers set us thirty-three to win. They were supremely confident but really, how can you lose with a snake-charmer on your side?

Apsarkhan, the nineteen-year-old who loved (you guessed it) Ricky Ponting and Sachin Tendulkar, was awarded Man of the Match. We also gave a cap to snake-charmer Aitram. The boys took us for a joy ride in their jeep afterwards, and Aitram celebrated by re-opening his picnic basket. The cobra didn't look happy. Later, I would discover that the trick to snake charming is to defang the poor buggers. A snake's venom is its saliva. Without saliva, like humans, it dies. The animal we had watched uncoil and struggle awkwardly would be dead in the next sixty to seventy days.

AMBER FORT, JAIPUR

INDIA

Sonu retired (had a customer to
   attend to) 0
Ali stumped Stew 14
Kanaya stumped Stew 0
Apsarkhan run out 14
Extras 5

TOTAL 33

BOWLING

Aitram 0-7, Justin 0-10, Stew 1-7,
  SK 2-11

BLACK CRAPS

Aitram bowled Raju 4
Justin not out 25
SK not out 7
Extras 1

TOTAL 37

BOWLING

Sonu 0-2, Kanaya 0-12, Apsarkhan 0-6,
  Raju 1-15

NEW ZEALAND WINS.
INDIA LEADS THE SERIES 5–4.

As the Goldfish Bowl departed, a phone beeped.

```
FROM JOHN BOUGEN:
JUST SPENT 3 HOURS BEING INTERROGATED BY EGYPTIAN JUDGE IN A ROOM
THE SIZE OF A TOILET. EVERYONE WAS SMOKING — I WAS IN HEAVEN.
```

Our final dinner in Jaipur was, for the most part, attended by three Black Craps. True to form, Brendon spent most of his meal visiting his favourite small room, barely able to finish a single sentence before having to leave again. Reece, ever the opportunist, asked on each occasion whether the patient would require the rest of his chips upon return. Proving he really did have a story for every occasion, Blanket Boy then proceeded to tell us of the dorm he stayed in once upon a time in Pakistan.

'I had the shits so bad,' he said, loading his plate with fries, 'I soiled every bed in the empty dorm, before having to do a runner.'

'How many beds were there?' I asked.

'Six or seven.'

'You're all class,' said Stew.

'Speaking of which,' continued Reece, looking at me, 'nice of you to hang your wet underpants on our veranda.'

'I had to,' I replied.

'Why?' asked Stew.

'It was a protest. You promised in Delhi that we'd get the best room in the next hotel. Isn't that right, Brendon?' But he was gone.

'Since you and Brendon both have young families,' said the understanding farmer, 'we've agreed to let you both have the executive room in Mumbai so at least you can have a sleep-in before returning to reality.'

The next hurdle was leaving the Pink City, banking on the fact that the F-word wouldn't affect our connecting flight from Delhi. It didn't, and next morning we were on our way to the city formerly known as Bombay. Much like Kolkata versus Calcutta or Myanmar versus Burma, it's intriguing when cities change names. In Mumbai's case, the city officially adopted its new handle in 1995 in an attempt to reclaim the city's Maratha heritage and break away from Bombay's associations with the Raj. 'Bombay,' however, remains in common usage, especially among the city's English-speaking residents. It must be a logistical nightmare — I get panicky enough changing an email address.

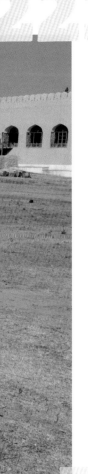

Amber Fort Jeep Drivers vs. the Black Craps. We beat them, but only because they had to work at the same time!

It was 32 degrees Centigrade, hot and clammy when Jet Airways touched down. And this was winter. Our taxi driver, who resembled a bearded Dustin Hoffman, informed us that there were only six weeks of the year where Mumbaikars don't have to tolerate rain, monsoons or oppressive heat. The latter was all too evident — my lower body felt as if it was on fire. Had this car, I wondered, ever been switched off?

'I have eight children,' Dustin said, chewing betel nut. 'Four boys, four girls.'

I unsuccessfully tried moving my seat back, the hairs on my legs feeling as if they were about to be singed. Dustin couldn't have been closer to the windscreen, nodding in time to nothing in particular.

'And how often do you work?' I asked.

'Seven days a week,' replied Dustin. 'Six am to midnight.'

We are so soft.

FOURTEEN

Previous page: Mumbai, the home of Bollywood and eighteen million residents, known locally as Mumbaikars. This fishing village near Nariman Point fails to cope with an overwhelming amount of waste.

A SECURITY RISK?

Traversing India is a drug, each city becoming the hit. Just when you think nothing can shock, another place slaps you square between the eyes. Mumbai is different again. Where Kolkata is the working-class brother who never gets the breaks, its west-coast equivalent is the younger, smarter, pushier one who scores the girls and cushy jobs. From its humble beginnings as a Portuguese fishing village in 1498, Bollywood's capital is now a juggernaut of trade, glamour, brashness and poverty. It's the LA of India, proudly pumping out nine hundred movies a year. It's also home to a million rickshaws and eighteen times as many people, a place where million-dollar apartments overlook million-population slums. While we're on numbers, despite Mumbai's unwelcome track record of slum dwellers, its literacy rate is 85.6 per cent (female 82.7 per cent, male 90 per cent) compared with India's overall rate of 65.4 per cent. And how about this: India boasts more billionaires than China but 81 per cent of its people live on less than two dollars a day, compared with 47 per cent of Chinese.

As we walked up to the hotel foyer, looking as though we'd had a squash workout, my room-mate and I, quite understandably, looked smug. We were, after all, about to score the room booked under Bougen for the final two nights. Finally, the two payers would get their just desserts while the freeloaders, who hadn't opened their wallets since Auckland, could experience cattle class. As we settled

into our executive room, my backpacker instincts kicked in. I dialled zero.

'Can you please tell me what extras an executive room gets?'

'You have wooden floors and two extra pieces of fruit,' said the woman.

I located the fruit bowl, which contained two apples and two bananas. Then the phone rang.

'Hey, wallah!'

'Yes, wallah?'

It was Reece. 'Thanks for swapping the booking.'

'No problem,' I said. 'We're enjoying the additional fruit and wooden floor.'

'Wait,' Reece said. 'So you didn't get your own room?'

'Course not.'

'Ha! We did.'

The tinny little bastards had done it again. Free trip. Best rooms. And whoops, sorry, seem to have left my credit card at home. Unbeknown to us, John had booked a single for his final night in India, which meant that Stew would also get a room to himself. As it stood, Blanket Boy, Brendon and I would have had to share a triple. Alas, as there were no spare triples, reception assumed that Brendon and I still wanted to share and so gave Reece, like Stew, his own room.

With a view.

Of palm trees and ocean.

'We've got a lot to learn,' I remarked to Brendon.

He shook his head in admiration. 'Bloody freeloaders.'

A comprehensively set field, accounting for every eventuality. Soon the police would arrive and spoil proceedings.

We met at reception some time later, refreshed and ready for Mumbai's onslaught. 'Let me take you out for lunch on Brendon's credit card,' said Reece, putting down his newspaper. We followed him through a jumble of street stalls and heat. Enterprising touts were selling chaat, savoury snacks; limu paani, lime juice; snazzy electronics; garish perfumes; and neke, shoes. Despite the temperature, not one local wore shorts. Just as were to about to accuse Reece of instigating a wild-goose chase, we stopped at an open-air restaurant in the tourist district of Colaba.

'This is Leopold's!' I said, seeing the name alongside the legend 'Since 1871'.

'Yep,' said Reece. 'Bit of a Mumbai institution.'

'But this is in the book I've been reading!'

'Have you finished that thing yet?' asked Stew.

'No, but this is the place!'

Leopold's was jam-packed but we fluked a table. Open twenty-four hours a day, this expat hang-out hummed with life. But was it heaving because of its reputation from

Muslim schoolboys dressed for the five-day form of the game. Chowpatty Beach, Mumbai.

Reece's days or, more likely, because of the recent bestseller? Had a once-cult restaurant become a Disney ride, as happened to the city of Savannah after *Midnight in the Garden of Good and Evil*? Did people come because of the book and, like me, did each customer expect each scene from its pages to unfold as we ate? Nothing did happen, of course. People ate and paid, like anywhere else. As we devoured delicious curry and beer, I saw ten copies of *Shantaram* piled up by the cash register.

At least they didn't have a gift shop.

Chowpatty Beach is Mumbai's centrepiece, a welcome breather from the lunacy of the inner city. Particularly popular on Sundays, it attracts families and sunset watchers. For the Black Craps, however, it meant a chance to play beach backyard cricket. But where was the action? The place was surprisingly devoid of people playing any kind of sport. Surely the home of Sachin Tendulkar hadn't transformed into a home of picnickers and kite flyers? Grown women played tag with their families, their saris trailing and bangles jangling as they did so, but that seemed to be the only action.

The only thing to do was start our own match. As usual, bat and ball in hand, we created attention by being our ridiculous selves. We found some school kids dressed in Muslim attire for Eid, and Reece begrudgingly took down their details. Two things hadn't changed: everyone fought and no one wanted to play for the Black Craps. We won the toss and sent India in. As the first ball was bowled, by a delightfully cheeky boy named Ibrar, literally hundreds of bystanders formed the largest slips cordon ever. The stumps, we decided, were to be a mostly limbless tree, which would also suffice as a wicketkeeper. The Arabian Sea, horrendously polluted, had third man covered. At fine leg were balloon sellers and chai boys, while ice-cream men looked after deep mid-wicket. Others, selling roasted nuts and corn, looked on from long off.

With all in readiness, a man who introduced himself as Noman Waghu told us, 'You can expect much humidity out here.' We thanked him for his concern. Then, barely two overs into the match, when Ibrar was bowling the spell of his life, a policeman parted the eager crowd and demanded our bat. 'No cricket!' he said, swiping the bat from India's opener, Amur.

'No cricket?' we asked, laughing nervously.

'No cricket, no football!'

And he confiscated our bat. The Black Craps, along with over a hundred

Mumbaikars, looked in wonder as he marched in silence, Vicky in one hand, and our Galaxy bat in the other, back to his post by the roadside.

'How about just a team photo with one of us holding the bat?' we asked.

'No,' he said, no doubt reckoning we would keep playing.

We trod lightly behind the policeman, following him to his post.

'No cricket, no soccer on the beach,' he repeated, not slowing down.

Once he reached his station by the promenade's footpath, two other policemen joined him. Both had perplexed looks on their faces, although nothing compared to ours.

'Do you want your bat back?' he asked, sounding like a stern father.

We resembled four boys who had hit their ball over the grumpy neighbour's fence one too many times. 'Yes, please,' I said, looking at my feet.

'Lots of people,' the policeman said, shaking his head. 'Security problem. There is terrorism in Mumbai. You mustn't play these games. Crowds are bad.'

Suddenly it all made sense, having read that morning that the terrorist attack on the Mumbai suburban railway in November 2006 was still being investigated. Two hundred and nine people lost their lives and more than seven hundred were injured in the attacks. According to the police, the bombings were carried out by

Lashkar-e-Taiba and Students Islamic Movement of India. All the bombs had been placed in the first-class 'general' compartments (some, called 'ladies' compartments, are reserved for women) of several trains running from the city-centre end of the railway line to the western suburbs. Home Minister Shivraj Patil told reporters that authorities had some information an attack was coming, 'but place and time was not known'.

This was our first match to be abandoned due to a security risk — a little more rock and roll than having a game called off by a town hall manager in Delhi. It did, however, hit home that even in the most scenic of surroundings, in India the fear of attack is always there.

till five-four down, we were no closer to clinching the Inaugural Indian Backyard Title. As it was, with just one day left, we would have to play for a drawn series. The heat was getting to us; we needed beer. We ordered three pitchers and a pepperoni pizza, feeling like arseholes because a beggar, no older than thirty, who appeared to have no lower body sat on the footpath outside our window. His lower torso just seemed to stop, as if the concrete path were quicksand and had swallowed his legs. His hands, his only way of getting about, were grey and scuffed. When we left, we gave him fifty rupees. His eyes lit up. Then he folded his toddler-sized legs into his chest and scrambled towards a busy intersection in a city that barely noticed.

Chowpatty Beach, Mumbai. Our first match to be called off due to our team being a security risk. 'No cricket! No soccer!'

Before bed, a text:

FROM JOHN BOUGEN:
IT'S EID. EVERY EGYPTIAN IS LEAVING EGYPT. I'M TRAPPED.

ow it was our last day in India, and we were determined to win our last game on Indian soil. Memories of Brijesh's match-fixing in Agra were still raw but, if nothing else, we were professional backyard cricketers. With the help of Kingfisher and Gordon's gin we were able to move on admirably. Perhaps the best preparation would be to visit the Cricket Club of India, the old stomping ground of John Wright, former coach of India — and Stew's cousin. One of the oldest and most prestigious cricket clubs in the country, the CCI was conceived as India's Marylebone Cricket Club, or MCC, and is every bit as exclusive and luxurious as the pompous beast itself.

Stew had a contact scribbled in his diary: President Mr Raj Singh Dungarpur.

CHOWPATTY BEACH, MUMBAI

INDIA

Mustaquim bowled Ibrar **0**
Nasim bowled Ibrar **2**

BOWLING

Ibrar 2-4, Jed 0-2

MATCH ABANDONED DUE TO SECURITY RISK.

We found him in a swanky office, filled with photos of Kapil Dev, Clive Lloyd, Gary Sobers, Ricky Ponting, Vivian Richards and Sachin Tendulkar, all of whom are honorary life members of an establishment fit for a Rajasthani prince.

Mr Dungarpur was a polite host, and impressed by Stew's royal cousin. 'John was a very good coach,' he said, showing us around a spotless stadium which, despite mostly being used for club games, would put most international equivalents to shame. Along with serving as the headquarters for the BCCI, the CCI had tennis courts, a swimming pool, fitness centres, a billiards room, squash courts, badminton courts, cafes, bars, a library and a reading room.

'I can see why Wrighty liked it here,' I whispered to Stew.

'Too right,' he replied.

On an outfield — a shade of green we hadn't seen since home — was a game between a Mumbai XI and a bunch of posh school kids from Kent, England. The latter were getting a hammering from their Indian counterparts, many of whom had clearly tasted first-class cricket. Mr Dungarpur sat us down on wicker chairs, more of which were being woven by hand in a nearby shady stand. We could handle the heat only long enough for a posed photo. Thankfully our host noticed,

Right: A rolled wicket — a luxury the Black Craps were never afforded while on tour in India. Oval Maidan, South Mumbai.

Below: A deceiving photo, portraying a calm, relaxed atmosphere. In reality, it was so hot we could only sit down for as long as it took to take the picture.

proudly moving indoors to a hallowed hallway carrying photographs of the world's hundred top cricketers. But you didn't have to play cricket to receive an honorary life membership: HRH Prince Philip and Ratan Tata (chairman of the Tata group, India's largest company) could also stay and play whenever they wished.

One obvious omission from the list was India's former coach himself. 'How come your cousin's not a life member?' I asked Stew. 'He's a god over here.'

'I don't know,' said Stew.

'Not good enough,' said Recce. 'He should be. And while you're at it, could you pull some strings and make us all life members?'

'Yeah,' I said, eyeing up the Wet Wicket bar. 'I could get used to this.'

'I don't think even Stew could bluff his way through that one,' said Brendon.

How fitting that our last game in India should echo our first. Mumbai's Oval Maidan, much like Kolkata's, covers a fair old chunk of land. The ground used to be owned and run by the state government and as a result was poorly maintained, and frequented by beggars, prostitutes and drug dealers. In 1997 the residents association stepped in and cleaned up its twenty-two acres, allowing

every cricket nut in town to bat where Tendulkar did. With the magnificent Mumbai High Court as a backdrop, we watched first-grade games take place in the maidan's centre. The players, dressed in white and competing on perfectly rolled pitches, were desperate to impress. On the ground's periphery, hackers, amateurs and hangers-on missed more balls than they hit.

'That's more like us,' I said, wiping my drenched brow.

'I agree,' said Stew. 'Let's get this thing over with before we die of heat exhaustion.'

Our opponents had bushy beards and an unhealthy disrespect for India. 'They'll probably be blowing shit up in twenty years,' said Reece as we watched the twenty-year-olds in question argue over a batting order.

It could have been the Mumbai heat, or the fear that our opponents might be carrying weapons, but nothing could hide the fact that the Black Craps saved their worst game for last. After Pakistan posted a score of fifty-one, we were just glad to be under shade. Normally backyard cricketers want to open the batting, but not in Mumbai's searing heat. For once, getting first bat was to draw the short straw.

When our innings at last began, Reece could barely keep up with the speed at which wickets fell. Stew missed a straight one and suddenly we had lost two wickets in two balls. I was facing a hat-trick. All those awful memories of getting bowled at school came flooding back. Keep it out, keep it out, I told myself. It would have made for a funnier story to be bowled first ball, but my ego couldn't stand it. This was only a game, but no one wants to be on the wrong end of a highlights package.

Alam came into bowl. He was swift and slippery, that much I had seen from Stew's innings. His teammates shouted to him, no doubt something along the lines of 'Get the sister fucker out!' He approached the bowling crease like a crazed fool. I tried to watch the ball leave his hand, doing my best not to visualise a death rattle and ensuing celebratory holler. The fielders moved in. The ball left Alam's hand. I didn't see it, just stuck my bat somewhere near its proposed destination. I hit it! I looked behind. It hadn't hit my stumps. Success! I belted the next delivery over long on for four, and was destined

Left: The lavish headquarters of the Cricket Club of India. A lifetime membership of 12 lakh (US$25,000) is waived if you happen to be Allan Border or Sunil Gavaskar.

Below: The Cricket Club of India has modelled itself on the MCC (Marylebone Cricket Club). Such a standard demands amenities such as hand-woven wicker chairs.

to become top scorer with a scorching half century and lead the Black Craps to victory, levelling a hard-fought series in award-winning, heroic, swashbuckling style.

The Black Craps' final match in India. We lost badly, but for once at least we chose an opening bowler with style. Oval Maidan, Mumbai.

If I hadn't been caught next ball.

Man of the Match was twenty-one-year-old Taffek Umar, fluent in Arabic and halfway through a degree at an Islamic polytech. Reece found it strange to meet Indians who adored Pakistan, yet despised their own country. Taffek confirmed this by saying that his favourite subject was Urdu and his favourite cricketer, most unlike an Indian fan to admit, was Pakistani power-hitter Shahid Afridi.

'Isn't it ironic,' mused Stew. 'Yesterday's game was abandoned because it was a terrorist risk, then we end up playing a group who want to be martyrs of Islam.'

'Yeah,' I said. 'And when they do blow something up, they'll do it wearing an Auckland Aces cap.'

Wink was a funky upmarket bar on the ground floor of our hotel. It had come highly recommended in *Time Out*. This was where India's elite drank cocktails, and where we spent our last few hours in India. Across the room, wealthy families kissed and laughed. One boy showed off his English girlfriend to his wary parents. We drank gin and toasted the town

OVAL MAIDAN, OPPOSITE HIGH COURT, MUMBAI

INDIA

Taffek Umar (capt) caught Mohammed
Asif **14**
Mohammed Alam retired **6**
Mozammil Hussen changed teams . . . **6**
Tofeek Kazza run out Mohammed
Asif **0**
Anser Riza not out **1**
Nazim Pasha not out **3**
Subahan Pasha caught Mohammed
Asif **4**
Taseem Nasar lbw Payaz **0**
Extras **17**

TOTAL. **51**

BLACK CRAPS

Stew bowled Mohammed Alam **3**
Justin caught Mohammed Alam **5**
Rajit Patel don't know how out, too
many quick wickets! **0**
Pappu Singh bowled Taseem **0**
Mohammed Asif run out Mohammed
Alam **6**
Payaz Alam don't know how out **0**
Extras **0**

TOTAL. **14**

BOWLING

Stew 1-9, Justin 0-9, Pappu Singh
0-21(!), Mohammed Asif 3-10, Payaz
Alam 1-4

INDIA WINS BY 37 RUNS.
INDIA WINS SERIES 5-4, WITH TWO
MATCHES ABANDONED.

otherwise known as 'London on acid'.

In the lift afterwards, I admitted to stealing a brown leather coaster with the bar's name on it. It came as little

These opponents had a creepy disrespect for India. Some were studying Arabic and Urdu, while others were reading the Koran. We imagined them becoming jihadists.

surprise to see the farmer confess the same, having smuggled one in his sock before departure. Reece nearly hit the roof upon rereading our bill for the evening. 'Two hundred and eighty dollars for six gins!' he exclaimed.

'They were doubles,' I said.

'Don't worry, it's Brendon's credit card, and he's in bed,' said Stew.

'That's the spirit,' I said.

'What a close-knit team,' Stew finished.

A phone sounded just as we reached our floor.

FROM JOHN BOUGEN:
YEEHAH! GOT LAST SEAT ON ONLY FLIGHT OUT OF EGYPT. DON'T CARE THAT
IT'S 3.40 AM VIA ABU DHABI.

T he next morning Stew read *The Times of India* in the lobby, cramming as many stories as possible. I looked around the hotel, doing the same with images and smells. Brendon had just returned from the toilet. It was 23 December and at home our families were lighting up the barbie and the Christmas tree. Reece was the only one of us staying on, opting to jump on a thirty-hour economy train ride back to Very-Nasty. He had his accommodation booked, but sadly not his second cousin's credit-card pin number. We had no time for breakfast, not that our bill included it, settling for stolen buns from the smorgasbord. Once a backpacker . . .

Outside, yellow Ambassadors came and went in Mumbai's early-morning haze. So did people. The sound of sweeping filled the air. Cars honked. Dogs barked. The city of eighteen million took a deep breath and prepared for chaos. Reece often spoke of what he missed about India when he returned to New Zealand: the element of danger and the sense that anything could happen. An uninsured builder would never balance on ten-storey-high scaffolding with a smile on his face in Tauranga. A family of five would be arrested for travelling on a moped in Wanganui. Our cotton-wool society protects us, but we do miss out on everyday adventure.

The breakfasts, the lunches and dinners. The piss-taking. The smell of piss. All things we would miss. John was the only one I had known before the trip started, yet because of that horrendous day in Varanasi he'd had to leave within days. For those of us left, it was an arranged marriage that worked. Guys don't gush and guys don't compliment, but after time in a frenzied whirlpool like India, a quiet respect had developed between all of us. We lived in each other's pockets, but no one flipped and no one grumbled. Maybe that was because each of us brought something to the table.

Stew had a way with people; kids, posh waiters, pushy touts. He was one of those rarest of animals: a traveller with no baggage. It helped, too, that the Indians were wary of his size and bald head. He would later say that he was astounded that no matter how chaotic things got in India, with every sense abused individually or all at once, to the locals it was just another day. 'A democratic society with room for obscene wealth and rejected lepers, all living together,' he said. 'But the best

thing, I reckon, has been the kids. They didn't know if they were poor, lucky, healthy or sick; they were just like their peers all around the world. The look on their faces when they bowled us out, or the cheek I was given when I took my hat off, would have been the same in Christchurch or Kolkata.'

Reece, for all his urine-guzzling and blanket-wearing, was a revelation. Never has 'don't judge a book by its cover' been more appropriate. He was the King of India, and we were envious. Those of us who speak only one language don't know how much we miss out on. For surely once you learn another, as Reece had, getting by on bastardised English in any multilingual nation must be like travelling with your ears, nose and eyes shut. His connection with Varanasi remained a mystery to us, but the love shown him by his adopted family on the Ganges was touching. 'I am constantly surprised that among such pandemonium, things still happen,' he'd said as we ground our way though Mumbai. 'And that Indians continue to be pretty chilled-out about everything.'

Brendon was the generous go-getter. It was he who, against all our wishes, determined we play one more game despite soaring temperatures. He could easily

have moaned the most, carrying that huge lens of his around town, but never did. While the rest of us bowled, argued and swore, he was more often than not perched on some nearby hilltop, doing his best to get the shot of the century. And he got more than a few. He should also be given points for tolerating would-be hackers when he's used to working with professional sportsmen. His transition from worry-free, scrounging tout to Dad was a smooth one, even if the rest of us abused the hell out of the privilege.

Soon, the familiar sight of the Goldfish Bowl rumbled into the hotel's forecourt. The big old tank would become home to another faceless group of shell-shocked travellers before we even reached Sahar International Airport. Encyclopaedic Farmer Guy continued to regurgitate facts from the paper. 'Did you know,' he said, incredulously, 'that Chandigarh, a city of only five million, has thirty-three thousand millionaires?'

'No I didn't.'

'And England were bowled out for eighty-one against Sri Lanka?'

'Is that right.'

The only piece missing from reception was Obi-Wan himself. Blanket Boy. Wallah. Gee. The Jedi Knight. As our driver prepared to load our bags, a lift bell chimed. The doors parted. Walking towards us was a man we knew well, but who somehow looked different. Almost naked, like a nun without her habit. Then we worked out why.

Nearly 90 per cent of commuters in Mumbai use public transport. Metered taxis are short on leg room, seat comfort, ceiling height and window space, but are ultimately more fun than their air-conditioned counterparts.

No blanket. T-shirt. And half-pants.

'You've changed,' Stew said, looking up from his paper.

'Only clean clothes I've got left.'

'Where's your respect, wallah?' I asked.

'You've corrupted me,' he confessed. 'I hope you're proud.'

'You may as well be nude,' said Brendon.

'Pretty unethical.'

'Are they swimming trunks? They are, aren't they!'

'Oh, get fucked,' said Reece. 'I've had enough of you lot.'

Man-hugs followed. Then Half-Pants Man went east to drink Old Monk by the Ganges while the rest of us went south, home for Christmas ham and backyard cricket.

Previous page: Love is ... a wall, some paint and a specially marked spot for wides.

O n 26 November, 2008 Mumbai was thrown into unprecedented chaos as militant gunmen took part of the city hostage. The attacks lasted three days and killed at least one hundred and seventy-three people, wounding nearly twice as many. I watched the horror unfold on CNN from our radio studio in Auckland as Indian reporters stood in front of plush hotels retelling indescribably cowardly acts perpetrated on their own people, as well as on innocent tourists.

Five days earlier, ten men had left Karachi, hijacked an Indian trawler and killed its captain. Then, with India's financial epicentre in sight, they stole three inflatable speedboats and prepared a deadly and terrifying assault. Armed with AK47 rifles, two of the terrorists entered the passenger hall of the Chhatrapati Shivaji Terminus railway station, opened fire and threw grenades, killing at least thirty people. Four men also entered the Taj Mahal Hotel, two entered the Oberoi Trident, and two entered Nariman House. Leopold's, the friendly expat hangout which features in *Shantaram* and where we ate curry and drank beer, was raided and ten people were shot.

India didn't deserve this. It is not a violent part of the world. That a country with over a billion people of many faiths should live in relative harmony most of the time says something about its inhabitants. I spoke to Stew during coverage of the attacks, and we reflected on what Reece had said about the Pakistan-loving Indians we'd played against in our last match in Mumbai: 'They'll be blowing shit up in twenty years.'

Mumbai continued to burn for days, its wounded recovering in hospitals, its dead mourned and celebrated through unusually quiet streets. TV coverage beamed images to the world. We had walked past those hotels. We had eaten in those restaurants. We had caught those trains. And when I asked each of the guys, each replied, just as I expected, 'I'd go back tomorrow.'

JOHN BOUGEN is now a farmer in the South Island high country. He didn't just fall in love with the land: he also tied the knot with author and farmer Christine Fernyhough, who had to forfeit the trip and give her ticket to Stew after she was charged by an angry heifer three weeks before departure date. John continues to hate Varanasi and love adventure.

REECE IRVING is currently finishing a Bachelor of Applied Science, majoring in environmental studies, in Tauranga. He still keeps in touch with the Black Craps and still eats with his fingers. His home is a hundred steps from the bottle store, where he speaks Hindi and reminisces about his first love with the equally homesick Indian owner. He no longer drinks his own urine.

BRENDON O'HAGAN hasn't put down his camera since returning home. Despite covering fashion and sports events, his experiences in India — watching an average team play averagely — haven't renewed his love for cricket one iota. He favours sharing a room with his wife over an intercontinental sleepwalker and, although it took months of dogged determination and bland food, his arse is now fine.

www.brendonohagan.co.nz

STEW GUNN was the only Black Crap to have a stopover at the conclusion of the tour. He says that his two days in Singapore were, compared to the madness of India, 'incredibly dull and uneventful'. He resumed life on his South Island farm, where he honks his tractor horn every couple of minutes to remind himself of Kolkata. He continues to wonder where his next freebie will come from.

AS FOR ME, I'm busy thinking about my next adventure. I drink a lot of chai with sugar and walk past my local curry house with a feeling of longing. I miss the country and I miss breakfasts with four blokes who showed no respect or pity for a man who suffered from somnambulism. India gets in your blood.

I bloody miss it.

www.justinbrownbooks.com

ACKNOWLEDGEMENTS
The Black Craps wish to acknowledge the following wonderful people at Random House for turning a crazy idea into a literary masterpiece: Nicola Legat, Anna Seabrook, Sarah Ell. Thanks to James Irving for your incredible patience and time. And lastly, and with much love, thanks to our long-suffering WAGS: Christine Fernyhough, Jess Gunn, Amy Malcolm, Sally O'Hagan . . . and Shanti.

A RANDOM HOUSE BOOK published by Random House New Zealand, 18 Poland Road, Glenfield, Auckland, New Zealand

For more information about our titles go to www.randomhouse.co.nz

A catalogue record for this book is available from the National Library of New Zealand

Random House New Zealand is part of the Random House Group
New York   London   Sydney   Auckland   Delhi   Johannesburg

First published 2009

The moral rights of the author have been asserted

ISBN 978 1 86979 155 1

Design: Anna Seabrook

Cover photograph: Brendon O'Hagan

Printed in China by Everbest Printing Co Ltd

JOHN BOUGEN